SEPHER YETZIRAH : THE BOOK OF FORMATION, AND THE THIRTY TWO PATHS OF WISDOM

FOLLOWED BY AN INTRODUCTION TO THE STUDY OF THE KABALAH

WILLIAM WYNN WESTCOTT

SCRIBERE SEMPER ET LEGERE

CONTENTS

INTRODUCTION 1

THE BOOK OF FORMATION

CHAPTER I 17
CHAPTER II 21
CHAPTER III 23
CHAPTER IV 26
CHAPTER V 30
CHAPTER VI 34

THE FIFTY GATES OF INTELLIGENCE 37
THE THIRTY-TWO PATHS OF WISDOM 42
Notes to the SEPHER YETZIRAH 49
Notes to the Thirty-Two Paths of Wisdom 66

AN INTRODUCTION TO THE STUDY OF THE KABALAH

Preface 71
1. The Kabalah 73
2. The Practical Kabalah 93
3. The Dogmatic Kabalah 103

SEPHER YETZIRAH : THE BOOK OF FORMATION, AND THE THIRTY TWO PATHS OF WISDOM

INTRODUCTION

The "Sepher Yetzirah," or "Book of Formation," is perhaps the oldest Rabbinical treatise of Kabalistic philosophy which is still extant. The great interest which has been evinced of late years in the Hebrew Kabalah, and the modes of thought and doctrine allied to it, has induced me to translate this tractate from the original Hebrew texts, and to collate with them the Latin versions of mediaeval authorities; and I have also published *An Introduction to the Kabalah* which may be found useful to students.

Three important books of the "Zohar," or "Book of Splendour," which is a great storehouse of Kabalistic teaching, have been translated into English by S. L. MacGregor Mathers, and the "Sepher Yetzirah" in an English translation is almost a necessary companion to these abstruse disquisitions: the two books indeed mutually explain each other.

The "Sepher Yetzirah," although this name means "The Book of Formation," is not in any sense a narrative of Creation, or a substitute Genesis, but is an ancient and instructive philosophical treatise upon one aspect of the origin of the universe and mankind; an aspect at once archaic and essentially Hebrew. The grouping of the processes of origin into an arrangement, at once alphabetic and numeral, is one only to be found in Semitic authors.

Attention must be called to the essential peculiarity of the Hebrew language, the inextricable and necessary association of numbers and letters; every letter suggesting a number, and every group of letters having a numerical signification, as vital as its literal meaning.

The Kabalistic principles involved in the reversal of Hebrew letters, and their substitution by others, on definite schemes, should also be studied and borne in mind.

It is exactly on these principles that the "groundwork idea" 'of this disquisition rests; and these principles may be traced throughout the Kabalistic tractates which have succeeded it in point of time and development, many of which are associated together in one volume known as the "Zohar," which is in the main concerned with the essential dignities of the Godhead, with the Emanations which have sprung therefrom, with the doctrine of the Sephiroth, the ideals of Macroprosopus and Microprosopus, and the doctrine of Re-incarnation.

The "Sepher Yetzirah," on the other hand, is mainly concerned with our universe and with the Microcosm. The opinions of Hebrew Kabalistic Rabbis and of modern mystics may be fitly introduced here.

The following interesting quotation is from Rabbi Moses Botarel, who wrote his famous Commentary in 1409:--"It was Abraham our Father--blessed be he--who wrote this book to condemn the doctrine of the sages of his time, who were incredulous of the supreme dogma of the Unity. At least, this was the opinion of Rabbi Saadiah--blessed be he--as written in the first chapter of his book *The Philosopher's Stone*. These are his words: The sages of Babylon attacked Abraham on account of his faith; for they were all against him although themselves separable into three sects. The First thought that the Universe was subject to the control of two opposing forces, the one existing but to destroy the other, this is dualism; they held that there was nothing in common between the author of evil and the author of good. The Second sect admitted Three great Powers; two of them as in the first case, and a third Power whose function was to decide between the two others, a supreme arbitrator. The Third sect recognised no god beside the Sun, in which it recognised the sole principle of existence."

Rabbi Judah Ha Lévi (who flourished about 1120), in his critical description of this treatise, wrote: "The Sepher Yetzirah teaches us the existence of a Single Divine Power by shewing us that in the bosom of variety and multiplicity there is a Unity and Harmony, and that such universal concord could only arise from the rule of a Supreme Unity."

According to Isaac Myer, in his *Quabbalah* (p. 159), the "Sepher Yetzirah" was referred to in the writings of Ibn Gebirol of Cordova, commonly called Avicebron, who died in A.D. 1070.

Eliphas Levi, the famous French Occultist, thus wrote of the "Sepher Yetzirah," in his *Histoire de la Magie*, p. 54: "The Zohar is a Genesis of illumination, the Sepher Jezirah is a ladder formed of truths. Therein are explained the thirty-two absolute signs of sounds, numbers and letters: each letter reproduces a number, an idea and a form; so that mathematics are capable of application to ideas and to forms not less rigorously than to numbers, by exact proportion and perfect correspondence. By the science of the Sepher Jezirah the human spirit is fixed to truth, and in reason, and is able to take account of the possible development of intelligence by the evolutions of numbers. The Zohar represents absolute truth, and the Sepher Jezirah provides the means by which we may seize, appropriate and make use of it."

Upon another page Eliphas Lévi writes: "The Sepher Jezirah and the Apocalypse are the masterpieces of Occultism; they contain more wisdom than words; their expression is as figurative as poetry, and at the same time it is as exact as mathematics.

In the volume entitled *La Kabbale* by the eminent French scholar, Adolphe Franck, there is a chapter on the "Sepher Yetzirah." He writes as follows:--

"The Book of Formation contains, I will not say system of physics, but of cosmology such as could be conceived at an age and in a country where the habit of explaining all phenomena by the immediate action of the First Cause, tended to check the spirit of observation, and where in consequence certain general and superficial relations perceived in the natural world passed for the science of Nature."...."Its form is simple and grave; there is nothing like a demonstration nor an argument; but it consists rather of a series of aphorisms, regularly grouped, and which have all the conciseness of the most ancient oracles."

In his analysis of the "Sepher Yetzirah," he adds:-- "The Book of Formation, even if it be not very voluminous, and if it do not altogether raise us to very elevated regions of thought, yet offers us at least a composition which is very homogeneous and of a rare originality. The clouds which the imagination of commentators have gathered around it, will be dissipated, if we look for, in it, not mysteries of ineffable wisdom, but an attempt at a reasonable doctrine, made when reason arose, an effort to grasp the plan of the universe, and to secure the link which binds to one common principle, all the elements which are around us."

"The last word of this system is the substitution of the absolute divine Unity for every idea of Dualism, for that pagan philosophy which saw in matter an eternal substance whose laws were not in accord with Divine Will; and for the Biblical doctrine, which by its idea of Creation, postulates two things, the Universe and God, as two substances absolutely distinct one from the other.

"In fact, in the 'Sepher Yetzirah,' God considered as the Infinite and consequently the indefinable Being, extended throughout all things by his power and existence, is while above, yet not outside of numbers, sounds and letters--the principles and general laws which we recognise."

"Every element has its source from a higher form, and all things have their common origin from the Word (*Logos*), the Holy Spirit.... So God is at once, in the highest sense, both the matter and the form of the universe. Yet He is not *only* that form; for nothing can or does exist outside of Himself; His substance is the foundation of all, and all things bear His imprint and are symbols of His intelligence."

Hebrew tradition assigns the doctrines of the oldest portions of the "Zohar" to a date antecedent to the building of the Second Temple, but Rabbi Simeon ben Jochai, who lived in the reign of the Emperor Titus, A.D. 70-80, is considered to have been the first to commit these to writing, and Rabbi Moses de Leon, of Guadalaxara, in Spain, who died in 1305, certainly reproduced and published the "Zohar."

Ginsburg, speaking of the Zoharic doctrines of the Ain Suph, says that they were unknown until the thirteenth century, but he does not deny the great antiquity of the "Sepher Yetzirah," in which it will be noticed the "Ain Suph Aur" and "Ain Suph" are not mentioned. I suggest, however, that this omission is no proof that the doctrines of "Ain Suph Aur" and "Ain Suph" did not then exist, because it is a reasonable supposition that the "Sepher Yetzirah" was the volume assigned to the Yetziratic World, the third of the four Kabalistic Worlds of Emanation, while the "Asch Metzareph" is concerned with the Assiatic, fourth, or lowest World of Shells, and is on the face of it an alchemical treatise; and again the "Siphra Dtzenioutha" may be fittingly considered to be an Aziluthic work, treating of the Emanations of Deity alone; and there was doubtless a fourth work assigned to the World of Briah--the second type, but I have not been able to identify this treatise. Both the Babylonian and the Jerusalem Talmuds refer to the "Sepher Yetzirah." Their treatise, named "Sanhedrin," certainly mentions the "Book of Formation," and another similar work; and Rashi in his commentary on the treatise "Erubin," considers this a reliable historical notice. Other historical notices are those of Saadya Gaon, who died A.D. 940, and Judah Ha Levi, A.D. 1150; both these Hebrew classics speak of it as a very ancient work. Some modern critics have attributed the authorship to the Rabbi Akiba, who lived in the time of the Emperor Hadrian, A.D. 120, and lost his life in supporting the claims of Barchocheba, a false messiah: others suggest it was first written about A.D. 200.

Graetz however assigns it to early Gnostic times, third or fourth century, and Zunz speaks of it as post Talmudical, and belonging to the Geonim period 700-800 A.D.; Rubinsohn, in the *Bibliotheca Sacra*, speaks of this latter idea as having no real basis.

The Talmuds were first collected into a concrete whole, and printed in Venice, 1520 A.D.

The "Zohar" was first printed in Mantua in 1558; again in Cremona, 1560; and at Lublin, 1623; and a fourth edition by Knorr von Rosenroth, at Sulzbach in 1684. Some parts are not very ancient, because the Crusades are mentioned in one chapter. Six extant Hebrew editions of the "Sepher Yetzirah" were collected and printed at Lemberg in 1680. The oldest of these six recensions was that of Saadjah Gaon (by some critics called spurious).There are still extant three Latin versions, *viz.*, that of Gulielmus Postellus; one by Johann Pistorius; and a third by Joannes Stephanus Rittangelius; this latter gives both Hebrew and Latin versions, and also "The Thirty-Two Paths" as a supplement.

There is a German translation, by Johann Friedrich von Meyer, dated 1830; a version by Isidor Kalisch, in which he has reproduced many of the valuable annotations of Meyer; an edition in French by Papus, 1888; an edition in French by Mayer Lambert, 1891, with the Arabic Commentary of Saadya Gaon; and an English edition by Peter Davidson, 1896, to which are added "The Fifty Gates of Intelligence" and "The Thirty-Two Ways of Wisdom." The edition which I now offer is fundamentally that of the ancient Hebrew codices translated into English, and collated with the Latin versions of Pistorius, Postellus, and Rittangelius, following the latter, rather than the former commentators. As to the authenticity of "The Sepher Yetzirah," students may refer to the *Bibliotheca magna Rabbinica* of Bartoloccio de Cellerio, Rome, 1678-1692; to Basnage, *History of the Jews*, 1708; and to *The Doctrine and*

Literature of the Kabalah, by A. B. Waite, 1902. The following copies of the "Sepher Yetzirah" in Hebrew, I have also examined, but only in a superficial manner:--

1. A Version by Saadiah, Ab. ben David, and three others, Mantua, 1562, 4to.

2. A Version with the commentary of Rabbi Abraham F. Dior, Amsterdam, 1642, 4to.

3. A Version with preface by M. ben J. Chagiz, Amsterdam, 1713, 16mo. 4. A Version, Constantinople, 1719, 8vo.

5. " " Zolkiew, 1745, 4to.

6. " " by Moses ben Jacob, Zozec, 1779, 4to.

7. " " Grodno, 1806, 4to.

8. " " Dyhernfurth, 1812, 8vo.

9. " " Salonica, 1831, 8vo.

10. A MS. copy dated 1719, in the British Museum.

I add here the full titles of the three Latin versions; they are all to be found in the British Museum Library.

"*Abrahami Patriarchae Liber Jezirah sive Formationis Mundi, Patribus quidem Abrahami tempora praecedentibus revelatus, sed ab ipso etiam Abra-*

hamo expositus Isaaco, et per pro prophetarum manus posteritati conservatus, ipsis autem 72 Mosis auditoribus in secundo divinae veritatis loco, hoc est in ratione, quoe est posterior authoritate, habitus." Parisiis, 1552. Gulielmus Postellus."Id est Liber Jezirah, qui Abrahamo, Patriarchae adscribitur, una cum Commentario Rabbi Abraham F.D. super 32 semitis Sapientiae, a quibus Liber Jezirah incipit: Translatus et notis illustratus a Joanne Stephano Rittangelio, Ling. Orient. in Elect. Acad. Regiomontana Prof. Extraord," Amstelodami, 1642. In Tomas Primus of "Artis Cabalisticae hoc est reconditae theologiae et philosophiae scriptorum." Basileae 1587, is found "Liber de Creatione Cabalistinis, Hebraice Sepher Jezira; Authore Abrahamo. Successive filiis ore traditus. Hinc jam rebus Israel inclinatis ne deficeret per sapientes Hierusalem arcanis et profundissimis sensibus literis commendatus." Johannes Pistorius.

The "Sepher Yetzirah" consists of six chapters, having 33 paragraphs distributed among them, in this manner: the first has 12, then follow 5, 5, 4, 3, and 4.

Yet in some versions the paragraphs and subject-matter are found in a different arrangement. The oldest title has, as an addition, the words, "The Letters of our Father Abraham" or "ascribed to the patriarch Abraham," and it is spoken of as such by many mediaeval authorities: but this origin is doubtless fabulous, although perhaps not more improbable than the supposed authorship of the "Book of Enoch," mentioned by St. Jude, of which two MSS. copies in the Ethiopic language were rescued from the wilds of Abyssinia in 1773 by the great traveller James Bruce. In essence this work was, doubtless, the crystallisation of centuries of tradition, by one writer, and it has been added to from time to time, by later authors, who have also revised it. Some of the additions, which were rejected even by mediaeval students, I have not incorporated with the text at all, and I present in this volume only the undoubted kernel of this occult nut, upon which many great authorities, Hebrew, German, Jesuit and others, have written long Commentaries, and yet have failed to explain satisfactorily. I find Kalisch, speaking of these Commentaries, says, "they contain nothing but a medley of arbitrary explanations, and sophistical distortions of scriptural verses, astrological notions, Oriental superstitions, a metaphysical jargon, a poor knowledge of physics, and not a correct elucidation of this ancient book." Kalisch, however, was not an occultist; these commentaries are, however, so extensive as to demand years of study, and I feel no hesitation in confessing that my researches into them have been but superficial. For convenience of study I have placed the Notes in a separate form at the end of the work, and I have made a short definition of the subject-matter of each chapter. The substance of this little volume was read as Lecture before "The Hermetic Society of London," in the summer of 1886, Dr. Anna Kingsford, President, in the chair. Some of the Notes were the explanations given verbally, and subsequently in writing, to members of the Society who asked for information upon abstruse points in the "Sepher," and for collateral doctrines; others, of later date, are answers which have been given to students of Theosophy and Hermetic philosophy, and to my pupils of the Study Groups of the Rosicrucian Society of England.

THE BOOK OF FORMATION

CHAPTER I

Section 1. In thirty-two [1] mysterious Paths of Wisdom did Jah, [2] the Jehovah of hosts, [3] the God of Israel, [4] the Living Elohim, [5] the King of ages, the merciful and gracious God, [6] the Exalted One, the Dweller in eternity, most high and holy--engrave his name by the three Sepharim [7] --Numbers, Letters, and Sounds. [8]

2. Ten are the ineffable Sephiroth. [9] Twenty-two are the Letters, the Foundation of all things; there are Three Mothers, Seven Double and Twelve [10] Simple letters.

3. The ineffable Sephiroth are Ten, as are the Numbers; and as there are in man five fingers over against five, so over them is established a covenant of strength, by word of mouth, and by the circumcision of the flesh. [11]

4. Ten is the number of the ineffable Sephiroth, ten and not nine, ten and not eleven. Understand this wisdom, and be wise by the perception. Search out concerning it, restore the Word to its creator, and replace Him who formed it upon his throne. (12)

5. The Ten ineffable Sephiroth have ten vast regions bound unto them; boundless in origin and having no ending; an abyss (13) of good and of ill; measureless height and depth; boundless to the East and the West; boundless to the North and South; (14) and the Lord the only God, (15) the Faithful King rules all these from his holy seat, (16) for ever and ever.

6. The Ten ineffable Sephiroth have the appearance of the Lightning flash, (17) their origin is unseen and no end is perceived. The Word is in them as they rush forth and as they return, they speak as from the whirl-wind, and returning fall prostrate in adoration before the Throne.

7. The Ten ineffable Sephiroth, whose ending is even as their origin, are like as a flame arising from a burning coal. For God (18) is superlative in his Unity, there is none equal unto Him: what number canst thou place before One.

8. Ten are the ineffable Sephiroth; seal up thy lips lest thou speak of them, and guard thy heart as thou considerest them; and if thy mind escape from thee bring it back to thy control; even as it was said, "run-

ning and returning" (the living creatures ran and returned) [19] and hence was the Covenant made.

9. The ineffable Sephiroth give forth the Ten numbers. First; the Spirit of the God of the living; [20] Blessed and more than blessed be the Living God [21] of ages. The Voice, the Spirit, and the Word, [22] these are the Holy Spirit.

10. Second; from the Spirit He produced Air, and formed in it twenty-two sounds--the letters; three are mothers, seven are double, and twelve are simple; but the Spirit is first and above these. Third; from the Air He formed the Waters, and from the formless and void [23] made mire and clay, and designed surfaces upon them, and hewed recesses in them, and formed the strong material foundation. Fourth; from the Water He formed Fire [24] and made for Himself a Throne of Glory with Auphanim, Seraphim and Kerubim, [25] as his ministering angels; and with these three [26] he completed his dwelling, as it is written, "Who maketh his angels spirits and his ministers a flaming fire." [27]

11. He selected three letters from among the simple ones and sealed them and formed them into a Great Name, I H V, [28] and with this He sealed the universe in six directions.

Fifth; He looked above, and sealed the Height with I H V.

Sixth; He looked below, and sealed the Depth with I V H.

Seventh; He looked forward, and sealed the East with H I V.

Eighth; He looked backward, and sealed the West with H V I.

Ninth; He looked to the right, and sealed the South with V I H.

Tenth; He looked to the left, and sealed the North with V H I.

12. Behold! From the Ten ineffable Sephiroth do, proceed--the One Spirit of the Gods of the living, Air, Water, Fire; and also Height, Depth, East, West, South and North. [29]

CHAPTER II

Section 1. The twenty-two sounds and letters are the Foundation of all things. Three mothers, seven doubles and twelve simples. The Three Mothers are Aleph, Mem and Shin, they are Air, Water and Fire Water is silent, Fire is sibilant, and Air derived from the Spirit is as the tongue of a balance standing between these contraries which are in equilibrium, reconciling and mediating between them.

2. He hath formed, weighed, and composed with these twenty-two letters every created thing, and the form of everything which shall hereafter be.

3. These twenty-two sounds or letters are formed by the voice, impressed on the air, and audibly modified in five places; in the throat, in the mouth, by the tongue, through the teeth, and by the lips. [31]

4. These twenty-two letters, which are the foundation of all things, He arranged as upon a sphere with two hundred and thirty-one gates, and the sphere may be rotated forward or backward, whether for good or for evil; from the good comes true pleasure, from evil nought but torment.

5. For He shewed the combination of these letters, each with the other; Aleph with all, and all with Aleph; Beth with all, and all with Beth. Thus in combining all together in pairs are produced the two hundred and thirty-one gates of knowledge. [32]

6. And from the non-existent [33] He made Something; and all forms of speech and everything that has been produced; from the empty void He made the material world, and from the inert earth He brought forth everything that hath life. He hewed, as it were, vast columns out of the intangible air, and by the power of His Name made every creature and everything that is; and the production of all things from the twenty-two letters is the proof that they are all but parts of one living body. [34]

CHAPTER III

Section 1. The Foundation of all the other sounds and letters is provided by the Three Mothers, Aleph, Mem and Shin; they resemble a Balance, on the one hand the guilty, on the other hand the purified, and Aleph the Air is like the Tongue of a Balance standing between them. (35)

2. The Three Mothers, Aleph, Mem and Shin, are a great Mystery, very admirable and most recondite, and sealed as with six rings; and from them proceed Air, Fire, and Water, which divide into active and passive forces. The Three Mothers, Aleph, Mem and Shin, are the Foundation, from them spring three Fathers, and from these have proceeded all things that are in the world.

3. The Three Mothers in the world are Aleph, Mem and Shin: the heavens [36] were produced [37] from Fire; the earth from the Water; and the Air from the Spirit is as a reconciler between the Fire and the Water.

4. The Three Mothers, Aleph, Mem and Shin, Fire, Water and Air, are shown in the Year: from the fire came heat, from the waters came cold, and from the air was produced the temperate state, again a mediator between them. The Three Mothers, Aleph, Mem and Shin, Fire, Water and Air, are found in Man: from the fire was formed the head; from the water the belly; and from the air was formed the chest, again placed as a mediator between the others.

5. These Three Mothers did He produce and design, and combined them; and He sealed them as the three mothers in the Universe, in the Year and in Man--both male and female. He caused the letter Aleph to reign in Air and crowned it, and combining it with the others He sealed it, as Air in the World, as the temperate (climate) of the Year, and as the breath in the chest (the lungs for breathing air) in Man: the male with Aleph, Mem, Shin, the female with Shin, Mem, Aleph. He caused the letter Mem to reign in Water, crowned it, and combining it with the others formed the earth in the world, cold in the year, and the belly in man, male and female, the former with Mem, Aleph, Shin, the latter

with Mem, Shin, Aleph. He caused Shin to reign in Fire, and crowned it, and combining it with the others sealed with it the heavens in the universe, heat in the year and the head in man, male and female. (38)

CHAPTER IV

Section 1. The Seven double letters, Beth, Gimel, Daleth, Kaph, Peh, Resh, and Tau have each two sounds associated with them. They are referred to Life, Peace, Wisdom, Riches, Grace, Fertility and Power. The two sounds of each letter are the hard and the soft--the aspirated and the softened. They are called Double, because each letter presents a contrast or permutation; thus Life and Death; Peace and War; Wisdom and Folly; Riches and Poverty; Grace and Indignation; Fertility and Solitude; Power and Servitude.

2. These Seven Double Letters point out seven localities; Above, Below, East, West, North, South, and the Palace of Holiness in the midst of them sustaining all things.

3. These Seven Double Letters He designed, produced, and combined, and formed with them the Planets of this World, the Days of the Week, and the Gates of the soul (the orifices of perception) in Man. From these Seven He hath produced the Seven Heavens, the Seven Earths, the Seven Sabbaths: for this cause He has loved and blessed the number Seven more than all things under Heaven (His Throne).

4. Two Letters produce two houses; three form six; four form twenty-four; five form one hundred and twenty; six form seven hundred and twenty; [39] seven form five thousand and forty; and beyond this their numbers increase so that the mouth can hardly utter them, nor the ear hear the number of them. So now, behold the Stars of our World, the Planets which are Seven; the Sun, Venus, Mercury, Moon, Saturn, Jupiter and Mars. The Seven are also the Seven Days of Creation; and the Seven Gateways of the Soul of Man--the two eyes, the two ears, the mouth and the two nostrils. So with the Seven are formed the seven heavens, [41] the seven earths, and the seven periods of time; and so has He preferred the number Seven above all things under His Heaven. [42]

Supplement to Chapter IV

NOTE.--This is one of several modern illustrations of the allotment of the Seven Letters; it is not found in the ancient copies of the "Sepher Yetzirah."

He produced Beth, and referred it to Wisdom ; He crowned it, combined and formed with it the Moon in the Universe, the first day of the week, and the right eye of man.

He produced Gimel, and referred it to Health; He crowned it, combined and joined with it Mars in the Universe, the second day of the week, and the right ear of man.

He produced Daleth, and referred it to Fertility; He crowned it, combined and formed with it the Sun in the Universe, the third day of the week, and the right nostril of man.

He produced Kaph, and referred it to Life; He crowned it, combined and formed with it Venus in the Universe, the fourth day of the week, and the left eye of man.

He produced Peh, and referred it to Power; He crowned it, combined and formed with it Mercury in the Universe, the fifth day of the week, and the left ear of man.

He produced Resh, and referred it to Peace; He crowned it, combined and formed with it Saturn in the Universe, the sixth day of the week, and the left nostril of man.

He produced Tau, and referred it to Beauty; He crowned it, combined and formed with it Jupiter in the Universe, the Seventh Day of the week, and the mouth of man.

By these Seven letters were also made seven worlds, seven heavens, seven earths, seven seas, seven rivers, seven deserts, seven days, seven weeks from Passover to Pentecost, and every seventh year a Jubilee.

Mayer Lambert gives:--Beth to Saturn and the Hebrew Sabbath--that is Saturday; Gimel to Jupiter and Sunday; Daleth to Mars and Monday; Kaph to the Sun and Tuesday; Peh to Venus and Wednesday; Resh to Mercury and Thursday; and Tau to the Moon and Friday.

CHAPTER V

Section 1. The Twelve Simple Letters are Héh, Vau, Zain, Cheth, Teth, Yod, Lamed, Nun, Samech, Oin, Tzaddi and Qoph; [43] they are the foundations of these twelve properties: Sight, Hearing, Smell, Speech, Taste, Sexual Love, Work, Movement, Anger, Mirth, Imagination, [44] and Sleep. These Twelve are also allotted to the directions in space: North-east, South-east, the East above, the East below, the North above, the North below, the South-west, the Northwest, the West above, the West below, the South above, and the South below; these diverge to infinity, and are as the arms of the Universe.

2. These Twelve Simple Letters He designed, and combined, and formed with them the Twelve celestial constellations of the Zodiac, whose signs are

Teth, Shin, Tau, Samech, Aleph, Beth, Mem, Oin, Qoph, Gimel, Daleth, and Daleth. [45] The Twelve are also the Months of the Year: Nisan, [46] Yiar, Sivan, Tamuz, Ab, Elul, Tishri, Hesvan, Kislev, Tebet, Sabat and Adar. The Twelve are also the Twelve organs of living creatures: [47] the two hands, the two feet, the two kidneys, the spleen, the liver, the gall, private parts, stomach and intestines.

He made these, as it were provinces, and arranged them as in order of battle for warfare. And also the Elohim [48] made one from the region of the other.

Three Mothers and Three Fathers; and thence issue Fire, Air and Water. Three Mothers, Seven Doubles and Twelve Simple letters and sounds.

3. Behold now these are the Twenty and Two Letters from which Jah, Jehovah Tzabaoth, the Living Elohim, the God of Israel, exalted and sublime, the Dweller in eternity, formed and established all things; High and Holy is His Name.

~

Supplement to Chapter V

NOTE.--This is a modern illustration of the allotment of the Twelve Letters; it is not found in the ancient copies of the "Sepher Yetzirah."

1. God produced Hé predominant in Speech, crowned it, combined and formed with it Aries in the Universe, Nisan in the Year, and the right foot of Man.

2. He produced Vau, predominant in mind, crowned it, combined and formed with it Taurus in the Universe, Aiar in the Year, and the right kidney of Man.

3. He produced Zain, predominant in Movement crowned it, combined and formed it with Gemini in the Universe, Sivan in the Year, and the left foot of Man.

4. He produced Cheth, predominant in Sight, crowned it, combined and formed it with Cancer in the Universe, Tammuz in the year, and the right hand of Man.

5. He produced Teth, predominant in Hearing, crowned it, combined and formed with it Leo in the Universe, Ab in the Year, and the left kidney in Man.

6. He produced Yod, predominant in Work, crowned it, combined and formed with it Virgo in the Universe, Elul in the Year, and the left hand of Man.

7. He produced Lamed, predominant in Sexual desire, crowned it, combined and formed with it Libra

in the Universe, Tishri in the Year, and the private parts of Man. (Kalisch gives "gall.")

8. He produced Nun, predominant in Smell, crowned it, combined and formed with it Scorpio in the Universe, Heshvan in the Year, and the intestines of Man.

9. He produced Samech, predominant in Sleep, crowned it, combined and formed with it Sagittarius in the Universe, Kislev in the Year, and the stomach of Man.

10. He produced Oin, predominant in Anger, crowned it, combined and formed with it Capricornus in the Universe, Tebet in the Year, and the liver of Man.

11. He produced Tzaddi, predominant in Taste, crowned it, combined and formed with it Aquarius in the Year, and the gullet in Man).

12. He produced Qoph, predominant in Mirth, crowned it, combined and formed with it Pisces in the Universe, Adar in the Year, and the spleen of Man.

NOTE.--Mediaeval authorities and modern editors give very different allocations to the twelve simple letters.

CHAPTER VI

Section 1. Three Fathers and their generations, Seven conquerors and their armies, and Twelve bounds of the Universe. See now, of these words, the faithful witnesses are the Universe, the Year and Man. The dodecad, the heptad, and the triad with their provinces; above is the Celestial Dragon, T L I, [49] and below is the World, and lastly the heart of Man. The Three are Water, Air and Fire; Fire above, Water below, and Air conciliating between them; and the sign of these things is that the Fire sustains (volatilises) the waters; Mem is mute, Shin is sibilant, and Aleph is the Mediator and as it were a friend placed between them.

2. The Celestial Dragon, T L I, is placed over the universe like a king upon the throne; the revolution

of the year is as a king over his dominion; the heart of man is as a king in warfare. Moreover, He made all things one from the other; and the Elohim set good over against evil, and made good things from good, and evil things from evil: with the good tested He the evil, and with the evil did He try the good. Happiness (50) is reserved for the good, and misery (51) is kept for the wicked.

3. The Three are One, and that One stands above. The Seven are divided; three are over against three, and one stands between the triads. The Twelve stand as in warfare; three are friends, three are enemies; three are life givers; three are destroyers. The three friends are the heart, the ears, and the mouth; the three enemies are the liver, the gall, and the tongue; (52) while God (53) the faithful king rules over all. One above Three, Three above Seven, and Seven above Twelve: and all are connected the one with the other.

4. And after that our father Abraham had perceived and understood, and had taken down and engraved all these things, the Lord most high (55) revealed Himself, and called him His beloved, and made a Covenant with him and his seed; and Abraham believed on Him (56) and it was imputed unto him for righteousness. And He made this Covenant as between the ten toes of the feet--this is that of circumcision; and as between the ten fingers of the hands and this is that of the

tongue. (57) And He formed the twenty-two letters into speech (58) and shewed him all the mysteries of them. (59) He drew them through the Waters; He burned them in the Fire; He vibrated them in the Air; Seven planets in the heavens, and Twelve celestial constellations of the stars of the Zodiac.

The End of "The Book of Formation

THE FIFTY GATES OF INTELLIGENCE

Attached to some editions of the "Sepher Yetzirah" is found this scheme of Kabalistic classification of knowledge emanating from the Second Sephira Binah, Understanding, and descending by stages through the angels, heavens, humanity, animal and vegetable and mineral kingdoms to Hyle and the chaos. The Kabalists said that one must enter and pass up through the Gates to attain to the Thirty-two Paths of Wisdom; and that even Moses only passed through the forty-ninth Gate, and never entered the fiftieth. See the *Oedipus Aegyptiacus* of Athanasius Kircher, vol. ii. p. 319.

First Order: Elementary.

1. Chaos, Hyle, The first matter.

2. Formless, void, lifeless.

3. The Abyss.

4. Origin of the Elements.

5. Earth (no seed germs).

6. Water.

7. Air.

8. Fire

9. Differentiation of qualities.

10. Mixture and combination.

Second Order: Decad of Evolution.

11. Minerals differentiate.

12. Vegetable principles appear.

13. Seeds germinate in moisture.

14. Herbs and Trees.

15. Fructification in vegetable life.

16. Origin of low forms of animal life.

17. Insects and Reptiles appear.

18. Fishes, vertebrate life in the waters.

19. Birds, vertebrate life in the air.
20. Quadrupeds, vertebrate earth animals.

Third Order: Decad of Humanity.
21. Appearance of Man.
22. Material human body.
23. Human Soul conferred.
24. Mystery of Adam and Eve.
25. Complete Man as the Microcosm.
26. Gift of five human faces acting exteriorly.
27. Gift of five powers to the soul.
28. Adam Kadmon, the Heavenly Man.
29. Angelic beings.
30. Man in the image of God.

Fourth Order: World of Spheres.
31. The Moon.
32. Mercury.
33. Venus.

34. Sol.

35. Mars.

36. Jupiter.

37. Saturn.

38. The Firmament.

39. The Primum Mobile.

40. The Empyrean Heaven.

Fifth Order: The Angelic World.

41. Ishim--Sons of Fire.

42. Auphanim--Cherubim.

43. Aralim--Thrones.

44. Chashmalim--Dominions.

45. Seraphim--Virtues.

46. Malakim--Powers.

47. Elohim--Principalities.

48. Beni Elohim--Angels.

49. Cherubim--Arch-angels.

Sixth Order: The Archetype.

50. God. Ain Suph. He Whom no mortal eye bath seen, and Who has been known to Jesus the Messiah alone.

NOTE.--The Angels of the Fifth or Angelic World are arranged in very different order by various Kabalistic Rabbis.

THE THIRTY-TWO PATHS OF WISDOM

Translated from the Hebrew Text of Joannes Stephanus Rittangelius, 1642: which is also to be found in the "Oedipus Aegyptiacus" of Athanasius Kircher, 1653.
(These paragraphs are very obscure in meaning, and the Hebrew text is probably very corrupt.)

The First Path is called the Admirable or the Hidden Intelligence (the Highest Crown): for it is the Light giving the power of comprehension of that First Principle which has no beginning; and it is the Primal Glory, for no created being can attain to its essence.

The Second Path is that of the Illuminating Intelligence: it is the Crown of Creation, the Splendour of the Unity, equalling it, and it is exalted above every head, and named by the Kabalists the Second Glory.

The Third Path is the Sanctifying Intelligence, and is the foundation of Primordial wisdom, which is called the Creator of Faith, and its roots are AMN; and it is the parent of Faith, from which doth Faith emanate.

The Fourth Path is named the Cohesive or Receptacular Intelligence; and is so called because it contains all the holy powers, and from it emanate all the spiritual virtues with the most exalted essences: they emanate one from the other by the power of the Primordial Emanation. The Highest Crown.) [1]

The Fifth Path is called the Radical Intelligence, because it resembles the Unity, uniting itself to the Binah, [2] or Intelligence which emanates from the Primordial depths of Wisdom or Chokmah. [3]

The Sixth Path is called the Mediating Intelligence, because in it are multiplied the influxes of the emanations, for it causes that influence to flow into all the reservoirs of the Blessings, with which these themselves are united.

The Seventh Path is the Occult Intelligence, because it is the Refulgent Splendour of all the Intellectual virtues which are perceived by the eyes of intellect, and by the contemplation of faith.

The Eighth Path is called the Absolute or Perfect Intelligence, because it is the means of the primordial, which has no root by which it can cleave, nor rest, except in the hidden places of *Gedulah*, [4] Magnificence, from which emanates its own proper essence.

The Ninth Path is the Pure Intelligence, so called because it purifies the Numerations, it proves and corrects the designing of their representation, and disposes their unity with which they are combined without diminution or division.

The Tenth Path is the Resplendent Intelligence, because it is exalted above every head, and sits on the throne of *Binah* (*the Intelligence spoken of in the Third Path*). It illuminates the splendour of all the lights, and causes an influence to emanate from the Prince of countenances. [5]

The Eleventh Path is the Scintillating Intelligence, because it is the essence of that curtain which is placed close to the order of the disposition, and this is a special dignity given to it that it may be able to stand before the Face of the Cause of Causes.

The Twelfth Path is the Intelligence of Transparency, because it is that species of Magnificence called Chazchazit, [6] the place whence issues the vision of those seeing in apparitions. (That is the prophecies by seers in a vision.)

The Thirteenth Path is named the Uniting Intelligence, and is so called because it is itself the Essence of Glory. It is the Consummation of the Truth of individual spiritual things.

The Fourteenth Path is the Illuminating Intelligence and is so called because it is that *Chashmal* [7] which is the founder of the concealed and fundamental ideas of holiness and of their stages of preparation.

The Fifteenth Path is the Constituting Intelligence, so called because it constitutes the substance of creation in pure darkness, and men have spoken of these contemplations; it is that darkness spoken of in Scripture, Job xxxviii. 9, "and thick darkness a swaddling band for it."

The Sixteenth Path is the Triumphal or Eternal Intelligence, so called because it is the pleasure of the Glory, beyond which is no other Glory like to it, and it is called also the Paradise prepared for the Righteous.

The Seventeenth Path is the Disposing Intelligence, which provides Faith to the Righteous, and they are clothed with the Holy Spirit by it, and it is called the Foundation of Excellence in the state of higher things.

The Eighteenth Path is called the Intelligence or House of Influence (by the greatness of whose abundance the influx of good things upon created beings is increased), and from its midst the arcana and hidden senses are drawn forth, which dwell in its shade and which cling to it, from the Cause of all causes.

The Nineteenth Path is the Intelligence of the Secret of all the activities of the spiritual beings, and is so called because of the influence diffused by it from the most high and exalted sublime glory.

The Twentieth Path is the Intelligence of Will, and is so called because it is the means of preparation of all and each created being, and by this intelligence the existence of the Primordial Wisdom becomes known.

The Twenty-first Path is the Intelligence of Conciliation and Reward, and is so called because it receives the divine influence which flows into it from its benediction upon all and each existence.

The Twenty-second Path is the Faithful Intelligence, and is so called because by it spiritual virtues are increased, and all dwellers on earth are nearly under its shadow.

The Twenty-third Path is the Stable Intelligence, and it is so called because it has the virtue of consistency among all numerations.

The Twenty-fourth Path is the Imaginative Intelligence, and it is so called because it gives a likeness to all the similitudes which are created in like manner similar to its harmonious elegancies.

The Twenty-fifth Path is the Intelligence of Probation, or Temptation, and is so called because it is the primary temptation, by which the Creator trieth all righteous persons.

The Twenty-sixth Path is called the Renewing Intelligence, because the Holy God renews by it all the changing things which are renewed by the creation of the world.

The Twenty-seventh Path is the Active or Exciting Intelligence, and it is so called because through it every existent being receives its spirit and motion.

The Twenty-eighth Path is called the Natural Intelligence; by it is completed and perfected the nature of all that exists beneath the Sun.

(*This Path is omitted by Rittangelius: I presume by inadvertence.*)

The Twenty-ninth Path is the Corporeal Intelligence, so called because it forms every body which is formed in all the worlds, and the reproduction of them.

The Thirtieth Path is the Collective Intelligence, and Astrologers deduce from it the judgment of the Stars and celestial signs, and perfect their science, according to the rules of the motions of the stars.

The Thirty-first Path is the Perpetual Intelligence; but why is it so called? Because it regulates the motions of the Sun and Moon in their proper order, each in an orbit convenient for it.

The Thirty-second Path is the Administrative Intelligence, and it is so called because it directs and associates the motions of the seven planets, directing all of them in their own proper courses.

NOTES TO THE SEPHER YETZIRAH

It is of considerable importance to a clear understanding of this Occult treatise that the whole work be read through before comment is made, so that the general idea of the several chapters may become in the mind one concrete whole. A separate consideration of the several parts should follow this general grasp of the subject, else much confusion may result.

This book may be considered to be an Allegorical Parallel between the Idealism of Numbers and Letters and the various parts of the Universe, and it sheds much light on many mystic forms and ceremonies yet extant, notably upon Freemasonry, the Tarot, and the later Kabalah, and is a great aid to the comprehension of the Astro-Theosophic schemes of the Rosicrucians. To obtain the full value of this Treatise, it should he studied hand in hand with Hermetic attributions, the "Isiac Tablet," and with a complete set of the designs, symbols and allocation of the Trump cards of the Tarot pack, for which see my translation of *The Sanctum Regnum of the Tarot*, by Eliphas Levi.

Note that the oldest MSS. copies of the "Sepher Yetzirah" have no vowel points: the latest editions have them. The system of points in writing Hebrew was not perfected until the seventh century, and even then was not in constant use. Ginsburg asserts that the system of vowel pointing was invented by a Rabbi Mocha in Palestine about A.D. 570, who designed it to assist his pupils. But Isaac Myer states that there are undoubted traces of pointing in Hebrew MSS. of the second century. According to A. E. Waite there is no extant Hebrew MSS. with the vowel points older than the tenth century.

The words "Sepher Yetzirah" are written in Hebrew from right to left, SPR YTzYRH, Samech Peh Resh, Yod Tzaddi Yod Resh Heh; modes of transliteration vary with different authors. Yod is variously written in English letters as I, Y, or J, or sometimes Ie. Tzaddi is property Tz; but some write Z only, which is misleading because the Hebrew has also a true Z, Zain.

CHAPTER I

The twelve sections of this chapter introduce this philosophic disquisition upon the Formation and Development of the Universe. Having specified the subdivision of the letters into three classes, the Triad, the Heptad, and the Dodecad, these are put aside for the time; and the Decad mainly considered as specially associated with the idea of Number, and as obviously composed of the Tetrad and the Hexad.

1. *Thirty-two.* This is the number of the Paths or Ways of Wisdom, which are added as a supplement. 32 is written in Hebrew by LB, Lamed and Beth, and these are the last and first letters of the Pentateuch. The number 32 is obtained thus--2 x 2 x 2 x 2 x 2=32. Laib, LB as a Hebrew word, means the Heart of Man.

*Paths.*The word here is NTIBUT, netibuth; NTIB meant primarily a pathway, or foot-made track; but is here used symbolically in the same sense as the Christian uses the word, *way*--the way of life: other meanings are--stage, power, form, effect; and later, a doctrinal formula, in Kabalistic writings.

2. *Jah.* This divine name is found in Psalm lxviii. 4; it is translated into Greek as *kurios*, and into Latin as *dominus*, and commonly into the English word,

Lord: it is really the first half of the word IHVH or Jehovah, or the Yahveh of modern scholars.

3. *Jehovah Tzabaoth*. This divine name is printed in English Bibles as Jehovah Sabaoth, or as "Lord of hosts" as in Psalm xxiv. 10. TzBA is an *army*.

4. *God of Israel*. Here the word God is ALHI, which in unpointed Hebrew might be God, or Gods, or My God.

5. *The Elohim of the Living*. The words are ALHIM ChIIM. Alhim, often written in English letters as Elohim, or by Godftey Higgins as Aleim, seems to be a masculine plural of the feminine form Eloah, ALH, of the divine masculine name EL, AL; this is commonly translated God, and means strong, mighty, supreme. Chiim is the plural of Chi--*living*, or *life*. ChIH is *a living animal*, and so is ChIVA. ChII is also *life*. Frey in his dictionary gives ChIIM as the plural word *lives*, or vitae. The true adjective for *living* is ChIA. Elohim Chiim, then, apart from Jewish or Christian preconception, is "the living Gods," or "the Gods of the lives, *i.e.,* living ones." Rittangelius gives Dii viventes, "The living Gods," both words in the plural. Pistorius omits both words. Postellus, the orthodox, gives Deus Vivus. The Elohim are the Seven Forces, proceeding from the One Divine, which control the "terra viventium," the manifested world of life.

6. *God.* In this case we have the simple form AL, EL.

7. *Sepharim.* SPRIM, the plural masculine of SPR, commonly translated *book* or *letter*: the meaning here is plainly "forms of expression."

8. *Numbers, Letters and Sounds.* The three Hebrew words here given are, in unpointed Hebrew, SPR, SPR and SIPUR. Some late editors, to cover the difficulty of this passage, have given SPR, SPUR, SIPR, pointing them to read Separ, Seepur, Saypar.

The sense of the whole volume appears to need their translation as Numbers, Letters and Sounds. Pistorius gave "Scriptis, numeratis, pronunciatis." Postellus gave "Numerans, numerus, numeratus," thus losing the contrasted meanings; and so did Rittangelius, who gave "Numero, numerante, numerato."

9. *The Ineffable Sephiroth.* The words are SPIRUT BLIMH, Sephiruth Belimah. The simplest translation is "the voices from nothing." The Ten Sephiruth of the Kabalah are the "Ten Primary Emanations from the Divine Source," which are the primal forces leading to all manifestation upon every plane in succession. Buxtorf gives for Sephiruth--predicationes logicae. The word seems to me clearly allied to the Latin spiritus--spirit, soul, wind; and is used by Quintilian as a sound, or noise. The meaning of *Belimah* is more doubtful. Rittan-

gelius always gives "praeter illud ineffabile." Pistorius gives "praeter ineffabile." Postellus evades the difficulty and simply puts the word Belimah into his Latin translation. In Frey's Hebrew Dictionary BLIMH is translated as *nothing*, without any other suggestion; BLI is "not," MR is "anything." In Kabalistic writings the Sephiruth, the Divine Voices and Powers, are called "ineffbilis," not to be spoken of, from their sacred nature.

10. The classification of the Hebrew letters into a Triad, Heptad and Dodecad, runs through the whole philosophy of the Kabalah. Many ancient authors added intentional blinds, suds as forming the Triad of A.M.T., Ameth, truth; and of AMN, Amen.

11. The Two Covenants, by the Word or Spirit, and by the Flesh, made by Jehovah with Abraham, Genesis xvii. The Covenant of Circumcision was to be an outward and visible sign of the Divine promise made to Ahraham and his offspring. The Hebrew word for circumcision is Mulah, MULH: note that MLH is also synonymous with DBR, dabar,--verbum or word.

12. Rittangelius gives "replace the formative power upon his throne." Postellus gives restore the device to its place."

13. *Abyss*; the word is OUMQ for OMQ, a depth, vastness, or valley.

14. My Hermetic rituals explained this Yetziratic attribution.

15. *The Lord the only God.* The words are ADUN IChID AL, or "Adonai (as commonly written) the only El."

16. *Seat.* The word is MOUN, dwelling, habitation, or throne.

17. *Lightning flash.* In the early edition the words "like scintillating flame" are used: the Hebrew word is BRQ. Many Kabalists have shown how the Ten Sephiroth are symbolised by the zig-zag lightning flash.

18. *God*; the Divine name here is Jehovah.

19. The text gives only RTzUAV ShUB--"currendo et redeundo," but the commentators have generally considered this to be a quotation from Ezekiel i. 14, referred to H ChIVT, the living creatures, kerubic forms.

20. The Spirit of the Gods of the Living. RUCh ALHIM ChIIIM; or as R. gives it, "spiritus Deorum Viventium." Orthodoxy would translate these words "The spirit of the living God."

21. AL ChI H OULMIM; "the Living God of Ages"; here the word God really is in the singular.

22. The Voice, Spirit and Word are QUL, RUCh, DBR. A very notable Hebrew expression of Divina-

tory intuition was BATh QUL, the Daughter of the Voice.

23. Formless and Void. THU and BHU; these two words occur in Genesis i. 2, and are translated "waste and void."

24. Note the order in which the primordial elements were produced. First, Spirit (query Akasa, Ether); then Air, Vayu; then Water, Apas, which condenses into solid elementary Earth, Prithivi; and lastly from the Water He formed Fire.

25. The first name is often written Ophanim, the letters are AUPNIM; in the Vision of Ezekiel i. 16, the word occurs and is translated "Wheels." ShRPIM are the mysterious beings of Isaiah vi. 2; the word otherwise is translated *Serpent*, and in Numbers xxi. 6, as "fiery serpents": also in verse 8 as "fiery serpent" when Jehovah said "Make thee a fiery serpent and set it upon a pole." Kerubim. The Hebrew words are ChIVTh H QDSh, holy animals: I have ventured to put Kerubim, as the title of the other Biblical form of Holy mysterious animal, as given in 1 Kings vi. 23 and Exodus xxv. 18, and indeed Genesis iii. 24. Bible dictionaries generally give the word as Cherubim, but in Hebrew the initial letter is always K and not Ch.

26. Three. In the first edition I overlooked this word *three*; and putting *and* for *as*, made four classes of serving beings.

27. This is verse 4 of Psalm civ.

28. Here follow the permutations of the name IHV, which is the Tetragrammaton--Jehovah, without the second or final Heh: IHV is a Trigrammaton, and is more suitable to the third or Yetziratic plane. HVI is the imperative form of the verb *to be*, meaning *be thou*; HIV is the infinitive; and VIH is future. In IHV note that Yod corresponds to the Father; Heh to Binah, the Supernal Mother; and Vau to the Microprosopus--Son.

29. Note the subdivision of the Decad into the Tetrad--four elements; and the Hexad--six dimensions of space.

CHAPTER 2

This chapter consists of philosophic remarks on the twenty-two sounds and letters of the Hebrew alphabet, and hence connected with the air by speech, and it points out the uses of those letters to form words--the signs of ideas, and the symbols of material substances.

30. *Soul*; the word is NPSh, which is commonly translated *soul*, meaning the living personality of man, animal or existing thing: it corresponds almost to the Theosophic Prana *plus* the stimulus of Kama.

31. This is the modern classification of the letters into guttural, palatal, lingual, dental and labial sounds.

32. *The 231 Gates.* The number 242 is obtained by adding together all the numbers from 1 to 22. The Hebrew letters can he placed in pairs in 242 different positions: thus *ab, ag, ad,* up to *at*; then *ba, bb, bg, bd,* up to *bt,* and so on to *ts, tt*: this is in direct order only, without reversal. For the reason why eleven are deducted, and the number 231 specified, see the Table and Note 15 in the edition of Postellus.

33. *Non-existent*; the word is AIN, nothingness. Ain precedes Ain Suph, boundlessness; and Ain Suph Aur, Boundless Light.

34. *Body*; the word is GUP, usually applied to the animal material body, but here means "one whole."

CHAPTER III

This chapter is especially concerned with the essence of the Triad, as represented by the Three Mothers, Aleph, Mem, and Shin. Their development in three directions is pointed out, namely in the Macrocosm or Universe; in the Year or in Time; and in the Microcosm or Man.

35. The importance of equilibrium is constantly reiterated in the Kabalah. The "Siphra Dtzeniouta,"

or "Book of Mystery," opens with a reference to this Equilibrium as a fundamental necessity of stable existence.

36. *Heavens.* The Hebrew word Heshamaim HSh-MIM, has in it the element of Aesh, fire, and Mim, water; and also Shem, name; *The* Name is IHVH, attributed to the elements. ShMA is in Chaldee a name for the Trinity (Parkhurst). ShMSh is the Sun, and Light, and a type of Christ, the Sun of Righteousness. Malachi iv. 2.

37. *Were produced.* The Hebrew word BRA, is the root. Three Hebrew words are used in the Bible to represent the idea of making, producing or creating.

BRIAH, Briah, giving shape, Genesis i. 1.

OShIH, Ashiah, completing, Genesis i. 31.

ITzIRH, Yetzirah, forming, Genesis ii. 7.

To these the Kabalists add the word ATzLH, with the meaning of "producing something manifest from the unmanifested."

38. These several formations then appear in a table thus :—

Emanation.	Shin.	Aleph.	Mem.
Macrocosm.	Primal Fire.	Spirit.	Primal Water.
Universe.	Heavens.	Atmosphere.	The Earth.
Elements.	Terrestrial Fire	Air.	Water & Earth
Man.	Head.	Chest.	Belly.
Year.	Heat.	Temperate.	Cold.

CHAPTER IV

This is the special chapter of the Heptad, the powers and properties of the Seven. Here again we have the threefold attribution of the numbers and letters to the Universe, to the Year, and to Man. The supplemental paragraphs have been printed in modern form by Kalisch; they identify the several letters of the Heptad more definitely with the planets, days of the week, human attributes and organs of the senses.

39. These numbers have been a source of difference between the editors and copyists, hardly any two editors concurring. I have given the numbers arising from continual multiplication of the product by each succeeding unit from one to seven. 2x1=2, 2x3=6, 6x4=24, 24x5=120, 120x6=720, 720x7=5040.

40. In associating the particular letters to each planet the learned Jesuit Athanasius Kircher allots Beth to the Sun, Gimel to Venus, Daleth to Mercury, Kaph to Luna, Peh to Saturn, Resh to Jupiter, and Tau to Mars. Kalisch in the supplementary paragraphs gives a different attribution; both are wrong, according to clairvoyant investigation. Consult the Tarot symbolism given by Court de Gebelin, Eliphas Levi, and my notes to the *Isiaic Tablet of Bembo*. The true attribution is probably not any-

where printed. The planet names here given are Chaldee words.

41. The Seven Heavens and the Seven Earths are printed with errors, and I believe intentional mistakes, in many occult ancient books. Some Hermetic MSS. have the correct names and spelling.

42. On the further attribution of these Seven letters, note that Postellus gives: Vita--mors, Pax--afflictio, Sapientia--stultitia, Divitiae (Opus)--paupertas, Gratia--opprobrium, Proles--sterilitas, Imperium--servitus. Pistorius gives: Vita--mors, Pax--bellum, Scientia--ignorantia, Divitiae--paupertas, Gratia--abominatio, Semen (Proles)--sterilitas, Imperium (Dominatio)--servitus.

CHAPTER V

This chapter is specially concerned with the Dodecad; the number twelve is itself pointed out, and the characters of its component units, once more in the three zones of the universe, year and man; the last paragraph gives a recapitulation of the whole number of letters: the Supplement gives a form of allotment of the several letters.

43. It is necessary to avoid confusion between these letters; different authors translate them in different manners. Heh or Hé not be confused with Cheth, or

Heth, Ch. Teth, Th also must be kept distinct from the final letter Tau, T, which is one of the double letters; the semi-English pronunciation of these two letters is much confused, each is at times both t and th; Yod is either I, Y, or J; Samech is simple S, and must not be confused with Shin, Sh, one of the mother letters; Oin is often written in English Hebrew grammars as Ayin, and Sometimes as Gnain; Tzaddi must not be confused with Zain, Z; and lastly Qoph, Q, is very often replaced by K, which is hardly defensible as there is a true K in addition.

44. Postellus gives *suspicion* and Pistorius, *mind*.

45. These letters are the initials of the 12 Zodiacal signs in Hebrew nomenclature. They are:

Teth	Telah	Aries	Mem	Maznim	Libra
Shin	Shor	Taurus	Oin	Oqereb	Scorpio
Tau	Thaumim	Gemini	Qoph	Qesheth	Sagittarius
Samech	Sartan	Cancer	Gimel	Gedi	Capricornus
Aleph	Aryeh	Leo	Daleth	Dali	Aquarius
Beth	Bethuleh	Virgo	Daleth	Dagim	Pisces

46. The month Nisan begins about March 29th. Yiar is also written Iyar, and Aiar: the Hebrew letters are AIIR.

47. The list of organs varies. All agree in two hands, two feet, two kidneys, liver, gall and spleen. Postellus then gives, intestina, vesica, arteriae," the intestines, bladder, and arteries; Rittangelius gives the same. Pistorius gives, "colon,

coagulum (spleen) et ventriculus," colon--the large intestine, coagulum and stomach. The chief difficulty is with the Hebrew word MSS, which is allied to two different roots, one meaning *private, concealed, hidden*; and the other meaning *liquefied*.

48. The Elohim--Divine powers--not IHVH the Tetragrammaton.

CHAPTER VI

This chapter is a *resumé* of the preceding five; it calls the universe and mankind to witness to the truth of the scheme of distribution of the powers of the numbers among created forms, and concludes with the narration that this philosophy was revealed by the Divine to Abraham, who received and faithfully accepted it, as a form of Wisdom under a Covenant.

49. The Dragon, TLI, Theli. The Hebrew letters amount in numeration to 440, that is 400, 30 and 10. The best opinion is that Tali or Theli refers to the 12 Zodiacal constellations along the great circle of the Ecliptic; where it ends there it begins again, and so the ancient occultists drew the Dragon with its tail in its mouth. Some have thought that Tali referred to the constellation Draco, which meanders across the Northern polar sky; others have referred it to the Milky Way; others to an imaginary

line joining Caput to Cauda Draconis, the upper and lower nodes of the Moon. Adolphe Franck says that Theli is an Arabic word.

50. *Happiness*, or a *good end*, or simply *good*, TUBH.

51. *Misery*, or an *evil end*, or simply *evil*, ROH.

52. This Hebrew version omits the allotment of the remaining six. Mayer gives the paragraph thus:-- The triad of amity is the heart and the two ears; the triad of enmity is the liver, gall, and the tongue; the three life-givers are the two nostrils and the spleen; the three death-dealing ones are the mouth and the two lower openings of the body.

53. *God*. In this case the name is AL, EL.

54. This last paragraph is generally considered to be less ancient than the remainder of the treatise, and by another author.

55. The Lord most high. OLIU ADUN. Adun or Adon, or Adonai, ADNI, are commonly translated *Lord*; Eliun, OLIUN, is the more usual form of "the most high one."

56. *Him*. Rittangelius gives "credidit in Tetragrammaton," but this word is not in the Hebrew.

57. *Tongue*. The verbal covenant.

58. *Speech*. The Hebrew has "upon his tongue."

59. The Hebrew version of Rabbi Judah Ha Levi concludes with the phrase, "and said of him, Before I formed thee in the belly, I knew thee." Rabbi Luria gives the Hebrew version which I have translated. Postellus gives: "He drew him into the water, He rose up in spirit, He inflamed him in seven suitable forms with twelve signs." Mayer gives: "Er zog sie mit Wasser, zundet sie an mit Feuer; erregte sie mit Geist; verbannte sie mit sieben, goss sie aus mit den zwolf Gestirnen." "He drew them with water, He kindled them with fire, He moved them with spirit, distributed them with seven, and sent them forth with twelve."

NOTES TO THE THIRTY-TWO PATHS OF WISDOM

1. The Highest Crown is Kether, the First Sephira, the first emanation from the Ain Suph Aur, the Limit-less Light.

2. Binah, or Understanding, is the Third Sephira.

3. Chokmah, Wisdom, is the Second Sephira.

4. Gedulah is a synonym of Chesed, Mercy, the Fourth Sephira.

5. Metatron, the Intelligence of the First Sephira, and the reputed guide of Moses.

6. This word is from ChZCh, a seer, seership. Chazuth is a vision.

7. This word means "scintillating flame."

The "Thirty-two Paths of Wisdom" refer to the Ten Sephiroth and the Twenty-two letters, each supplying a type of divine power and attributes. In my *Introduction to the Kabalah* will be found a diagram showing how the Paths from Eleven to Thirty-two connect the several Sephiroth, and are deemed to transmit the divine influence. Some teachers of Occult Science also allot the Twenty-two Trumps of the Tarot Cards to the twenty-two Paths.

AN INTRODUCTION TO THE STUDY OF THE KABALAH

PREFACE

Students of literature, philosophy and religion who have any sympathy with the Occult Sciences may well pay some attention to the Kabalah of the Hebrew Rabbis of olden times; for whatever faith may be held by the enquirer he will gain not only knowledge, but also will broaden his views of life and destiny, by comparing other forms of religion with the faith and doctrines in which he has been nurtured, or which he has adopted after reaching full age and powers of discretion.

Being fully persuaded of the good to be thus derived, I desire to call attention to the dogmas of the old Hebrew Kabalah. I had the good fortune to be attracted to this somewhat recondite study, at an early period of life, and I have been able to spare a little time in subsequent years to collect some knowledge of this Hebrew religious philosophy; my information upon the subject has been enlarged by my membership of The Rosicrucian Society.

Yet the Kabalistic books are so numerous and so lengthy, and so many of them only to be studied in Rabbinic Hebrew and Chaldee that I feel to-day less confident of my knowledge of the Kabalah than I did twenty years ago, when this essay was first published, after delivery in the form of lectures to a Society of Hermetic Students in 1888.

Since that date a French translation of "The Zohar," by Jean de Pauly, and a work entitled "The Literature and History of the Kabalah," by Arthur E. Waite, have been published, yet I think that this little treatise will be found of interest to those who have not sufficient leisure to master the more complete works on the Kabalah.

The Old Testament has been of necessity referred to, but I have by intention made no references to the New Testament, or to the faith and doctrines taught by Jesus the Christ, as the Saviour of the world: if any desire to refer to the alleged reference in the Kabalah to the Trinity, it will be found in the Zohar ii., 43, b.: and an English version of the same in "The Kabbalah," by C. D. Ginsburg.

WM. WYNN WESTCOTT, M.B., etc.

1

THE KABALAH

It must be confessed that the origin of the Kabalah is lost in the mists of antiquity; no one can demonstrate who was its author, or who were its earliest teachers.

Considerable evidence may be adduced to show that its roots pass back to the Hebrew Rabbis who flourished at the time of the Second Temple about the year 515 B.C. Of its existence before that time I know of no proofs.

It has been suggested that the captivity of the Jews in Babylon led to the formation of this philosophy by the effect of Chaldean lore and dogma acting on Jewish tradition. No doubt in the earliest stages of its existence the teaching was entirely oral, hence the name QBLH from QBL to receive, and it became varied by the minds through which it filtered in its course; there is no proof that any part of it was written for centuries after. It has been kept curiously distinct both from the Exoteric Pentateuchal Mosaic books, and from the ever-growing Commentaries upon them, the Mishna and Gemara, which form the Talmud. This seems to have grown up in Hebrew theology without combining with the recondite doctrines of the Kabalah. In a similar manner we see in India that the Upanishads, an Esoteric series of treatises, grew up alongside the Brahmanas and the Puranas, which are Exoteric instructions designed for the use of the masses of the people.

With regard to the oldest Kabalistic books still extant, a controversy has raged among modern critics, who deny the asserted era of each work, and try to show that the assumed author is the only person who could not have written each one in question. But these critics show the utmost divergence of opinion the moment it becomes necessary to fix on a date or an author; so much more easy is destructive criticism than the acquirement of real knowledge.

Let us make a short note of the chief of the old Kabalistic treatises.

The "Sepher Yetzirah" or "Book of Formation" is the oldest treatise; it is attributed by legend to Abraham the Patriarch: several editions of an English translation by myself have been published. This work explains a most curious philosophical scheme of Creation, drawing a parallel between the origin of the world, the sun, the planets, the elements, seasons, man and the twenty-two letters of the Hebrew alphabet; dividing them into a Triad, a Heptad and a Dodecad; three mother letters A, M, and Sh are referred to primeval Air, Water and Fire; seven double letters are referred to the planets and the sevenfold division of time, etc.: and the twelve simple letters are referred to the months, zodiacal signs and human organs. Modern criticism tends to the conclusion that the existing ancient versions were compiled about A.D. 200. The "Sepher Yetzirah" is mentioned in the Talmuds, both of Jerusalem and of Babylon; it was written in the Neo-Hebraic language, like the Mishna.

The "Zohar" or" Sohar" spelled in Hebrew ZHR or ZUHR "The Book of Splendour" or of "Light," is a collection of many separate treatises on the Deity, Angels, Souls and Cosmogony. Its authorship is ascribed to Rabbi Simon ben Jochai, who lived A.D. 160; he was persecuted and driven to live in a cave by Lucius Aurelius Verus, co-regent with the Emperor Marcus Aurelius Antoninus. Some considerable portion of the work may have been arranged by him from the oral traditions of his time: but other parts have certainly been added by other hands at intervals up to the time when it was first published as a whole by Rabbi Moses de Leon, of Guadalajara in Spain, circa 1290. From that time its history is known; printed Editions have been issued in Mantua, 1558, Cremona, 1560, and Lublin, 1623; these are the three famous Codices of "The Zohar" in the Hebrew language. For those who do not read Hebrew the only practical means of studying the Zohar are the partial translation into Latin of Baron Knorr von Rosenroth, published in 1684 under the title of "Kabbala Denudata"; and the English edition of three treatises,--"Siphra Dtzenioutha" or "Book of Concealed Mystery"; "Ha Idra Rabba," "Greater Assembly"; and "Ha Idra Suta," " Lesser Assembly," translated by S. L. MacGregor Mathers. These three books give a fair idea of the tone, style and material of the Zohar but they only include a partial view: other tracts in the Zohar are :--Hikaloth--The Palaces, Sithre Torah--Mysteries of the Law, Midrash ha Neelam--The secret commentary, Raja Mehemna—The faithful shepherd, Saba Demishpatim,--The discourse of the Aged--the prophet Elias, and Januka-- The Young man; with Notes called Tosephta and Mathanithan.

In course of publication there is now a French translation of the complete Zohar, by Jean de Pauly: this is a most scholarly work.

Other famous Kabalistic treatises are :-- "The Commentary on the Ten Sephiroth," by Rabbi Azariel ben Menachem, 1200 A.D. ; "The Alphabet" of

Rabbi Akiba; "The Gate of Heaven"; the "Book of Enoch"; "Pardes Rimmonim, or Garden of Pomegrantes"; "A treatise on the Emanations"; "Otz ha Chiim, or The Tree of Life" of Chajim Vital; "Rashith ha Galgulim, or Revolutions of Souls" of Isaac de Loria; and especially the writings of the famous Spanish Jew, Ibn Gebirol, who died A.D. 1070, and was also called Avicebron, his great works are "The fountain of life" and "The Crown of the Kingdom."

The teaching of the Kabalah has been considered to be grouped into several schools, each of which was for a time famous. I may mention :--The School of Gerona, 1190 to 1210, of Rabbi Isaac the Blind, Rabbis Azariel and Ezra, and Moses Nachmanides. The School of Segovia of Rabbis Jacob, Abulafia (died 1305), Shem Tob (died 1332), and Isaac of Akko. The School of Rabbi Isaac ben Abraham Ibn Latif about 1390. The School of Abulafia (died 1292) and Joseph Gikatilla (died 1300); also the Schools of "Zoharists" of Rabbis Moses de Leon (died 1305), Menahem di Recanti (died 1350), Isaac Loria (died 1572) and Chajim Vital, who died in 1620. A very famous German Kabalist was John Reuchlin or Capnio, and he wrote two great works, the "De Verbo Mirifico," and "De arte Cabalistica."

In the main there were two tendencies among the Kabalists: the one set devoted themselves entirely to the doctrinal and dogmatic branch: the other to the practical and wonder-working aspect.

The greatest of the wonder-working Rabbis were Isaac Loria, also called Ari; and Sabatai Zevi, who curiously enough became a Mahommedan. Both of these departments of Occult Rabbinic lore have their living representatives, chiefly scattered individuals; very rarely groups of initiates are found. In Central Europe, parts of Russia, Austria and Poland there are even now Jews, known as Wonderworking Rabbis, who can do strange things they attribute to the Kabalah, and things very difficult to explain have been seen in England, at the hands of students of Kabalistic rites and talismans.

The Rabbinic Commentaries, many series deep, overlaying each other, which now exist in connection with the old treatises form such a mass of Kabalistic lore as to make it an almost impossible task to grasp them; probably no Christian nor Jew in this country can say what doctrines are not still laid up in some of the old manuscript works.

The Dogmatic or Theoretical Kabalah indicates philosophical conceptions respecting the Deity, Angels and beings more spiritual than man; the human Soul and its several aspects or parts; concerning pre-existence and re-incarnation and the several worlds or planes of existence.

The Practical Kabalah attempts a mystical and allegorical interpretation of the Old Testament, studying each phrase, word and letter; it teaches the connection between letters and numbers and the modes of their inter-relation; the principles of Gematria, Notaricon, and Temura; the formation and uses of the divine and angelic names as Amulets; the formation of Magic Squares; and a vast fund of allied curious lore, which subsequently formed the basis of Mediaeval Magic.

For those who do not wish to read any Kabalistic work as a whole, but rather to glean a general view of this philosophy, there are now three standard works; two are in English; one by Dr. C. Ginsburg, 1865, a formal and concise resume of the doctrines; the other, an excellent book, "The Doctrine and Literature of the Kabalah," by Arthur E. Waite, 1902; and one in French by Adolph Franck, 1889, which is more discursive and gives fewer details.

Many points of the teaching of Indian systems of religious philosophy are not touched on by the Hebrew system, or are excluded by differences of a fundamental nature: such as the Cosmogony of other Worlds, unless the destroyed Worlds of Unbalanced Force refer to these; the inviolability of law, as Karma, is not a prominent feature; Reincarnation is taught, but the number of re-births is limited generally to three.

Some small part of the Kabalistic doctrine is found in the Jewish Talmud, but in that collection of treatises there is some grossness that is absent from the true Kabalah; such are the theories of the debasement of men into animal forms; and of men to be reborn as women, as a punishment for earthly sins in a previous life.

It must be remembered that many points of doctrine are limited to the teachings of but a few Rabbis; and that the differences between the earliest and latest doctrines on a given point are sometimes very great, as is shown by a comparison of the Books of the Rabbis of different eras and schools. Some of the Kabalistic teaching has also never been printed nor published, and has been handed down even to this day from master to pupil only: there are some points not found in any Hebrew book, which I myself have taught in the Rosicrucian Society and in Hermetic Lodges. An attentive study of some of these old mystical Hebrew books discloses the existence of intentional "blinds," which appear to have been introduced to confine certain dogmas to certain students fitted to receive them, and to preserve them from promiscuous distribution and so from misuse by the ignorant or vicious.

Two or three centuries have now passed since any notable addition to the body of Kabalistic doctrine has been made, but before that time a long succession of commentaries had been produced, all tending to illustrate or extend the philosophical scheme.

As already said, when the Kabalah first took shape as a concrete whole and a philosophic system, may remain for ever an unknown datum, but if we regard it, as I believe is correct, as the Esotericism of the religion of the Hebrews, the foundation dogmas are doubtless almost as old as the first promulgation of the main principles of the worship of Jehovah.

I cannot now attempt any glance at the contentions of some doubting scholars, who question whether the story of the Twelve Tribes is a historic fact, or whether there ever were a Moses, or even a King Solomon. It is sufficient for the present purpose that the Jewish nation had the Jehovistic theology and a system of priestly caste, and a coherent doctrine, at the time of the Second Temple when Cyrus, Sovereign of all Asia, 536 B.C., holding the Jews in captivity, permitted certain of them to return to Jerusalem for the express purpose of reestablishing the Hebrew mode of worship which had been forcibly interfered with by Nebuchadnezzar in 587 B.C.

After this return to Jerusalem it was that Ezra and Nehemiah, circa 450 B.C., edited and compiled the Old Testament of the Hebrews, or according to those who deny the Mosaic authorship and the

Solomonic regime, it was then that they wrote the Pentateuch.

The renewed worship maintained until 320 B.C., when Jerusalem was captured by Ptolemy Soter, who, however, did not destroy the foundations of the Jewish religion; indeed his successor, Ptolemy Philadelphus, caused the Hebrew scriptures to be revised and translated into Greek by Seventy-two scholars, about 277 B.C.; this has been known for centuries as the Septuagint version of the Old Testament.

Further Jewish troubles followed, however, and Jerusalem was again taken and pillaged by Antiochus in 170 B.C. Then followed the long wars of the Maccabees; subsequently the Romans dominated Judea, then quarrelling with the Jews the city was taken by Pompey, and not long after was again plundered by the Roman general Crassus in 54 B.C. Yet the Jewish religion was preserved, and we find the religious feasts and festivals all in progress at the time of Jesus; yet once more in A.D. 70, was the Holy City taken, plundered and burnt, and that by Titus, who became Emperor of the Romans in A.D. 79.

Through all these vicissitudes, the Hebrew Old Testament survived, yet must almost unavoidably have had many alterations and additions made to its several treatises; the more Esoteric doctrines which were handed down along the line of the priestly caste, and not incorporated with the Torah offered to the people, may no doubt have been repeatedly varied by the influences of contending teachers.

Soon after this period was framed the first series of glosses and commentaries on the Old Testament books, which have come down to our times. Of these the earliest are the volume called the "Targum of Onkelos" on "The Law," written about A.D. 100, and that of Jonathan ben Uzziel on "The Prophets."

About A.D 141 there first came into note the now famous treatise written by the Rabbis of Judah, called "Mishna," and this formed the basis of those vast compilations of Hebrew doctrine called the "Talmud," of which there are two extant forms, one compiled at Babylon-the most notable, and the other associated with Jerusalem. To the original "Mishna" the Rabbis added further commentaries named "Gemara." From this time the literature of Judaism grew apace, and there was a constant succession of notable Hebrew Rabbis who published religious treatises, until at least A.D. 1500. The two Talmuds were first printed at Venice in 1520 and 1523 respectively.

The Old Testament books were the guiding light through the ages of the Jews, but the learned Rabbis were not satisfied with them alone, and they supplemented them by two parallel series of works of literature; the one, Talmudic, being commentaries based upon Thirteen Rules of Argument delivered by Moses to illustrate the Old Testament, and supply material for teaching the populace; and the other a long series of treatises of a more abstruse character, designed to illustrate their Secret Doctrines and Esoteric views. The Sepher Yetzirah, and the Zohar or Book of Splendour represent the kernel of that oral instruction which the Rabbis of the olden times prided themselves upon possessing, and which they have even claimed as being "The Secret Knowledge" which God gave to Moses for the use of the priests themselves, in contradistinction to the Written Law intended for the masses of the people.

One of the principal conceptions of the Kabalah is that spiritual wisdom is attained by Thirty-two Paths, typified by the Ten numbers and the Twenty-two letters; these Ten again being symbols of the Divine Emanations, the Sephiroth, the Holy Voices chanting at the Crystal Sea, the Great Sea, the Mother Supernal, Binah; and of the Twenty-two occult forces of the Nature of the Universe symbolised by the Three primary Elements, the Seven Planets, and the Twelve Zodiacal influences of the heavens, which tincture human concerns through the path of our Sun in its annual course. I have given the names and definitions of the Thirty-two Paths at the end of my Edition of the" Sepher Yetzirah."

Now to show the close connection between the Kabalah and orthodox Judaism, we find the Rabbis cataloguing the Books of the Old Testament into a series of Twenty-two (the letters) works to be read for the culture of spiritual life; this Twenty-two they obtained from the Thirty-nine books of the O.T. Canon, by collecting the twelve minor prophets into one treatise; Ruth they added to Judges; Ezra to Nehemiah; while the two books each of Samuel, Kings, and Chronicles, they called one each. The Canon of Thirty-nine works was fixed in the time of Ezra.

Returning to the books which illustrate the Kabalah, whatever may be the authenticity of their alleged origins, it cannot be denied that those ancient volumes, Sepher Yetzirah and Zohar, contain a system of spiritual philosophy of clear design, deep intuition and far-reaching cosmologic suggestions; that are well worthy of the honour of receiving a special name and of founding a theological body of doctrine,--The Kabalah.

The bulwark and main foundation of the public Hebrew religion has always been the Pentateuch, five treatises attributed to Moses, which proclaim the Laws of Jehovah given to his chosen people. The Old Testament beginning with these five books is further continued by historic books, by poetical teachings and by prophetic works, but many portions are marked by materialistic characteristics and a lack of spiritual rectitude which the books of a Great Religion might be expected to display, and they even offend our present standard of moral life.

The Mosaic Law, eminently valuable for many purposes to a small nation 3,000 years ago, and containing many regulations of a type showing great attention to sanitary matters, is yet marred by the application of penalties of gross cruelty and harsh treatment of erring mortals, which are hardly compatible with our modern views of what might have emanated from God the personal Creator of this Universe with its million worlds; and the almost entire absence of any reference to a life after death for human beings shows a materialism which needed a new Revelation by Jesus, whose life has earned the title of "Christ." Yet the orthodox of England hear this statement with incredulity, and if asked to show the passages in the Old Testament which insist on a life after death, or on a succession of lives for purposes of retribution, or the passages demonstrating the immortality of the soul, they could not produce them, and are content to refer you to the clergy, whose answer generally is, "If not plainly laid down, these dogmas are implied." But are they? If they are, how is it that notably clear passages can be quoted which show that important authors in the Old Testament make statements in direct opposition to these doctrines? And how is it, again, that a great author of modern times has said, "Prosperity was the blessing of the Old Testament for good works, but adversity that of the New"? This could only be true if there were no future life or lives, or no coming period of reward and punishment contemplated by the Old Testament doctrine.

But the comment is true and the Old Testament does teach that man is no more immortal than the beast, as witness Ecclesiastes, iii. 19 :--"For that which befalleth the sons of men, befalleth beasts; even one thing befalleth them: as the one dieth, so dieth the other; yea they have all one breath; so that man hath no pre-eminence above a beast: for all is vanity. All go unto one place; all are of the dust, and all turn to dust again. . . . Wherefore I perceive that there is nothing better, than that a man should rejoice in his own works; for that is his portion: for who shall bring him to see what shall be after him?" Who, indeed, except his own Ego, Soul or Higher Self.

But perhaps this book is from the pen of some obscure Jew, or half pagan Chaldee or Babylonian. Not at all: Jewish critics have all assigned it to Solomon, who was the King of the Jews at the time of their heyday of glory; surely if the immortality of the soul were the essence of the Judaism of the people, Solomon could not have so grossly denied it.

Go back, however, to the narrative of Creation in Genesis, and the same story is found; the animals are made from the dust, man is made from the dust, and Eve is made from Adam, and each has breathed into the form, the "Nephesh Chiah,"--the breath of life, vitality; but there is no hint that Adam received a Ray of the Supernal Mind, which was to dwell there for a time, to gain experience, to receive retribution, and then enter another stage of progress, and achieve a final return to its Divine source. And yet the authors of these volumes, whoever they were, could hardly have been without the conception of the higher part of man, of his Spiritual Soul. The critical contention is that the Old Testament was deprived at some period of its religious philosophy, which was set apart for a privileged class; while the husk of strict law and tradition was alone offered for the acceptance of the people. The kernel of spiritual philosophy which is lacking in the Old Testament as a religious book may be the essential core of the Kabalah; for these Kabalistic dogmas are Hebraic, and they are spiritual, and they are sublime in their grandeur; and the Old Testament read by their light becomes a volume worthy of the acceptance of a nation. I speak of the essentials of the Kabalah, the ancient substratum of the Kabalah. I grant that in many extant treatises these primal truths have been obscured by generations of editors, by visionary and often crude additions, and by the vagaries of Oriental imagery; but the keynotes of a great spiritual Divine concealed Power, of its Emanations in manifestation, of its energising of human life, of the prolonged existence of human souls, and of the temporary state of corporeal existence, are fundamental doctrines there fully illustrated; and these are the points of contact between the Kabalah of the Jew and the so-called Esotericism of the teachings of Buddha and of Hinduism.

It may be that the Catholic Church, from which the Protestant Church seceded, was from its origin in the possession of the Hebrew Rabbinic secret of the intentional Exoteric nature of the Bible, and of a priestly mode of understanding the Esoteric Kabalah, as a key to the true explanations of the Jewish books, which being apparently histories are really largely allegorical. If this were granted, it would explain why the Catholic Church has for ages discouraged the laity from the study of the Old Testament books, and would lead us to think that Protestantism made a mistake in combining with the Reformation of a vicious priesthood the encouragement of the laity to read the Old Testament books.

I note that the literal interpretation of the Mosaic books and those of the Old Testament generally has repeatedly been used as a support for vicious Systems of conduct; a notable example of which was seen even a hundred years ago, when the clergy of Protestant nations almost unanimously supported the continuance of the Slave Trade from arguments derived from the laws of Jehovah as stated to have been compulsory upon the Jews.

The Freethinkers of that day were largely the champions of suffering and oppressed races, and for centuries the wisest of men, the greatest scientists have maintained, and ever won, struggle after struggle with the assumed infallibility of old Hebraic Testament literal instructions, assertions and narratives.

The Old Testament may indeed be, to some extent, the link which binds together thousands of Christians, for Jesus the Christ founded His doctrine upon a Jewish people, but the interminable list of Christian sects of to-day have almost all taken their rise from the assertion of a right of personal interpretation of the Bible, which might have remained debarred to the generality by the confession that the keys of interpretation were lost, or at least missing, and that without their assistance error of a vital character was inevitable.

The vast accumulation of varying interpretations of the Bible, although a folly, yet sinks into insignificance as an incident of importance, before the collateral truth that the followers of each of the hundreds of sects have arrogated to themselves, not only the right of personal interpretation, but the duty of condemning all others--as if the infallibility they claimed for the Bible could not fail to be reflected upon their personal propaganda, or the specialities of a chapel service. Religious intolerance has cursed every village of the land, and hardly a single sect has originated which has not only claimed the right to differ from others, and to criticise, but also to persecute and assign to perdition all beyond its own narrow circle.

The Mystic, the Occultist and the Theosophist do indeed do good, or God, service, by illustrating the bases and origins of all faiths by the mutual illumination that is available. By tolerance and mutual esteem much good may arise, but by the internecine struggles of religionists, every faith is injured, and religion becomes a by-word meaning intolerance, strife and vainglory, and the mark and profession of an earnest sectarian is now that he is ever ready to condemn the efforts of others, in direct opposition to the precept of Jesus the Christ, Who said--"Judge not, that ye be not judged."

One sect of the Jews, the Caraites, successors of the Sadducees, throughout history rejected the Kabalah, and it is necessary to say here that the Hebrew Rabbis of this country of the present day do not follow the practical Kabalah, nor accept all the doctrines of the Dogmatic Kabalah. On the other hand, many famous Christian authors have expressed great sympathy with the Doctrinal Kabalah.

St. Jerome, who died in A.D. 420, in his "Letter to Marcella," gives us all the Kabalistic Divine Names allotted to the Ten Sephiroth. Others were Raymond Lully, 1315; Pope Sixtus the Fourth, 1484; Pic de Mirandola, 1494; Johannes Reuchlin, 1522; H. Cornelius Agrippa, 1535; Jerome Cardan, 1576; Gulielmus Postellus, 1581; John Pistorius, 1608; Jacob Behmen, 1624; the notable English Rosicrucian, Robert Fludd, 1637; Henry More, 1687; the famous Jesuit Athanasius Kircher, 1680; and Knorr von Rosenroth, 1689. To these must be added Eliphaz Levi and Edouard Schure, two modern French writers on the Occult Sciences, and two English authors, Anna Kingsford and Edward Maitland. The notable German philosopher Spinoza, 1677, regarded the doctrines of the Kabalah with great esteem.

2

THE PRACTICAL KABALAH

Let us take the Practical Kabalah before the Dogmatic; it may perhaps have preceded the Theoretical Philosophy because it was at first concerned with an intimate study of the Pentateuch; a research based upon the theory that every sentence, word and letter were given by Divine Inspiration and that no jot or tittle (the Yod the smallest Hebrew letter) must be neglected. The Rabbis counted every word and letter, and as their numbers were represented by their letters, they counted the numeration of all God names and titles, and all proper names, and the numeration of the phrases recording Divine commands.

The Hebrew letters and numbers were :

Aleph	A	1
Beth	B, V	2
Gimel	G, Gh	3
Daleth	D, Dh	4
Heh	H	5
Vau	O, U, V	6
Zayin	Z	7
Cheth	Ch	8
Teth	T	9
Yod	I, Y	10
Kaph	K, Kh	20
Lamed	L	30
Mem	M	40
Nun	N	50
Samekh	S	60
Ayin	Aa, Ngh	70
Pe	P	80
Tzaddi	Tz	90
Qoph	Q	100
Resh	R	200
Shin	Sh	300
Tau	T, Th	400

There were also several final letters, final K, 500; final M, 600; final N, 700; final P, 800; and final Tz, 900. Note that the Divine Name Jah, JH, numbered 15, and so in common usage the number 15 was always represented by 9 and 6, ThV, Teth and Vau.

The Kabalistic Rabbis granted the natural meaning of the words of the "Torah" or Law books of the Old Testament as a guide to a knowledge of proper conduct in life and as a proper reading for the Synagogue and home but they claimed that each verse and narrative, each law and incident, had also a deeper and concealed meaning of a Mystical character to be found by their calculations, conversions, and substitutions, according to their rules of Gematria, Notaricon, and Temura: the first name is of Greek origin, the second from the Latin, but the third was Hebrew and meant permutation, TMURH, from the root MUR,--changed.

The most famous Rabbi of the Seventeenth century named Menasseh ben Israel, compared the Books of Moses to the body of a man, the commentaries called Mishna to the soul, and the Kabalah he called the Spirit of the soul: "ignorant people may study the first, the learned the second, but the wisest direct their contemplation to the third"; he called the Kabalists,--divine theologians possessed of thirteen rules by which they are enabled to penetrate the mysteries with which the Scriptures abound.

Many Kabalists claimed that their doctrines and methods were brought down from Heaven by Angels to primeval man, and they all believed that the First Four Books of the Pentateuch enshrined their peculiar doctrines as well as narrated histories and laid down laws.

The Zohar says :--If these books of the Torah contain only the tales of, and the words of Esau, Hagar,

Laban and Balaam, why are they called--The Perfect Law, The Law of Truth, The True Witness of God?--there must be a hidden meaning. "Woe be to the man who says that The Law (Torah) contains only common sayings and tales: if this were true we might even in our time compose a book of doctrine which would be more respected. No, every word has a sublime sense, and is a heavenly mystery. The Law resembles an angel: to come down on earth a spiritual angel must put on a garment to be known or understood here, so the Law must have clothed itself in a garment of words as a body for men to receive; but the wise look within the garments."

At some periods both the ordinary Jew and even Christian Fathers have made a somewhat similar declaration of a literal and a mystical meaning of scripture. The Talmud in book "Sanhedrin" remarks that Manasseh King of Israel asked whether Moses could not relate something of more value than tales of Timnah a concubine, and Rachel with her mandrakes, and he is answered that there is a concealed meaning in these narrations.

The Christian Father Origen (A.D. 253), in his "Homilies," wrote that everybody should regard these stories, the making of the world in six days, and the planting of trees by God,--as figures of speech under which a recondite sense is concealed. Origen granted a Three-fold meaning,--somatic, psychic, and pneumatic; or the body of scripture, its soul and its spirit.

Nicholas de Lyra who died in 1340 accepted four modes of interpretation; literal, allegoric, moral, and anagogic or mystical.

In this he nearly follows the scheme of the Zohar ii. 99: in which paragraph there is a parable comparing the Sacred Law to a woman in love who reveals herself to her friend and beloved: first by signs, ramaz; then by whispered words, derush; then by converse with her face veiled, hagadah; and at last she reveals her features and tells all her love, this is sod, association in secret, a mystery.

The late Dr. Anna Kingsford and Edward Maitland were notable Kabalists who always insisted on the concealed meanings underlying the ordinary sense of the old Hebrew writings; and the late H.P. Blavatsky used to declare that the truly ancient texts of ancient religions were susceptible of explanations on seven planes of thought.

The Kabalists discovered deep meanings in each Hebrew letter, common and finals, and found secrets in large letters, misplaced letters and in words spelled in unusual manners. At different times they represented God by an Aleph, A; or by a Yod, I; or by a Shin; or by a Point; or by a Point within a circle; or even by a Triangle; and by a Decad of ten yods.

GEMATRIA was a mode of interpretation by which a name or word having a certain numerical value was deemed to have a relation with some other words having the same number; thus certain numbers became representative of several ideas, and were considered to be interpretative one of the other. For example, Messiah spelled, MShICh, numbered 358, and so does the phrase IBA ShILH, Shiloh shall come; and so this passage in Genesis 49 V. 10, was considered to be a prophesy of the Messiah: note that Nachash, NChSh, the Serpent of Moses, is also 358. The letter Shin, Sh, 300, became an emblem of divinity by corresponding with Ruach Elohim, RUCh ALHIM, the Spirit of the Living God.

NOTARICON, or abbreviation, is of two forms; one word is formed from the initial and final letters of one or more words; or the letters of one name are taken as the initials or finals of the words of a sentence. For example, in Deut. 30 V. 12, Moses asks, Who shall go up for us to Heaven? The initial letters of the original words MI IOLH LNV HSh-MILH, form the word MILH, mylah, which word means circumcision, and the final letters are IHVH, the name Jehovah: hence it was suggested that circumcision was a feature of the way to God in heaven.

Amen, AMN is from the initials of Adonai melekh namen. "The Lord and faithful king"; and the famous Rabbinic word of power used for talismans AGLA is formed of the initials of the words "Ateh gibur leolam Adonai," "The Lord ever powerful," or Tu potens in saeculum Dominine.

TEMURA is a more complex procedure and has led to an immense variety of curious modes of divination: the letters of a word are transposed according to certain rules and with many limitations: or again, the letters of a word are replaced by other letters as arranged by a definite scheme, often shown in a diagram. For example, a common form was to write one half of the alphabet over the other in reverse order, and so the first letter A was replaced by the last T, and B by Shin, and so on. On this plan the word Sheshak of Jeremiah 25 v. 26, is said to mean Babel: this permutation was known as ATBSh, atbash. On this principle we find twenty-one other possible forms named in order Albat, Abgat, Agdat: the complete set was called "The combinations of Tziruph." Other forms were rational, right, averse and irregular, obtained from a square of 22 spaces in each direction, that is of 484 secondary squares, and then putting a letter in each square in order up and down, and then reading across or diagonally, etc. Of this type is the so-called "Kabalah of Nine Chambers" of the Mark Masons.

A further development of the numerical arts was shown by the modes of Contraction and Extension; thus Jehovah, IHVH 26, was extended to IVD-HA-

VV-HA, and so 10, 5, 6, 5 or 26 became 20, 6, 12, 6 or 44. By extension Zain, Z.7, became 1, 2, 3, 4, 5, 6 and 7 or 28; or 28 was regarded as 2 and 8 or 10. The Tetragrammaton, Jehovah 26 was also at times regarded as 2 and 6 or 8: so El Shaddai, God Almighty, AL ShDI, 1, 30, 300, 4, 10, was 345 and then 12 and then 3, a Trinity. A quaint conceit was that of the change of the spelling of the names of Abraham and Sara: at first Abram ABRM and Sarai ShRI, became ABRHM and ShRH: they were 100 and 90 years old and were sterile: now H, Heh, was deemed of a fertile type, and so the letter H was added to ABRAM, and the Yod I, converted into an H of the name Sarai.

In the very old "Sepher Yetzirah" is found the allocation of letters to the planets; from this origin arose a system of designing talismans written on parchment or engraved on brass or gems: as each planet had a letter and a number, in regard to each was allotted a Magic Square of lesser squares; thus for Jupiter 4 was the number and Daleth the letter, and the Magic Square of Jupiter had 16 smaller squares within it; in each a number 1 to 16, and so each line added up to 34 and the total of numbers was 136. Every Talisman duly formed bore at least one God name to sanctify it: notable names were IH, Jah; ALH, Eloah; then IHVH; then the notable 42 lettered Name, which was really composed of others,--

Aheie asher aheie (I am that I am) Jah, Jehuiah, Al, Elohim, Jehovah, Tzabaoth, Al Chai and Adonai.

The Shemhamphorash, or Separated Name, was a famous Word of Power; it was formed of Three times 72 letters: the words of three verses, 19, 20 and 21 of Exodus XIV. were taken: the separated letters of verse 19 were written down, then the letters of verse 20 in reverse order, then those of verse 21 in direct order: this gave 72 Names read from above down, each of 3 letters: to each was added either AL or IH, and so were formed the names of the 72 Angels of the Ladder of Jacob which led from earth to heaven: these names were often placed on the obverse and reverse of medals or rolls of parchment to form 36 Talismans.

According to some Kabalists both King David and King Solomon were able to work wonders with Kabalistic Magical Arts: The Pentagram was called the Seal of Solomon, and the Hexagram was called the Shield of David; to the points of the former were assigned the Spirit and Four Elements, while to those of the latter were ascribed the Planets. The treatise called "The Clavicules of King Solomon" is of course a mediaeval fraud.

The Hebrew letters are also associated with the Twenty-two Trumps of the Tarot pack of cards; these cards have been much used for purposes of divination. The Gipsies of Southern Europe use these cards for Fortune-telling. The French author Court de Gebelin (1773-1782) declared that these Trump cards as mystical emblems were derived from the magic of Ancient Egypt. Occult Science allots each card to a Number, a Letter and a natural object or force,-the Planets, Zodiacal signs, elements, etc. "The Sanctum Regnum of the Tarot Trumps" edited by myself can be consulted. Dr. Encausse of Paris, who writes under the pseudonym of "Papus," has also a work relating to the Tarots and gives a Kabalistic attribution of the Trump cards which Rosicrucians consider to be erroneous.

So far as is known to me the practice of Kabalah as a Magical Art is now almost restricted to Russian and Polish Rabbis, and to a few students of occultism in this country, some of whom constantly wear a Kabalistic talisman although they are Christians.

3

THE DOGMATIC KABALAH

"The great doctrines of the Theoretical Kabalah," says Ginsburg, "are mainly designed to solve the problems of (a) the nature of the Supreme Being, (b) the creation of the Universe and of our world, (c) the creation of angels and man, (d) the destiny of the world and of men, and (e) the import of the revealed law."

The Kabalah confirms the following Old Testament declarations: the Unity of God, His incorporeal form (Deut. chap. iv., v. 15.); eternity, immutability, perfection and goodness; the origin of the world at God's will, the government of the Universe, and the creation of man after the image of God. It seeks to explain by Emanations the transition from the Infinite to the finite, the multitude of forms from a unity; the production of matter from spiritual intelligence; and the relations existing between Creator and creature. In this theosophy,--ex nihil nihilo fit; spirit and matter are the opposite poles of one existence: and as nothing comes from nothing, so nothing is annihilated.

The following seven Kabalistic ideals are of the greatest interest to students of the origin and destiny of the world and mankind.

(1) That God, the Holy One, the Supreme Incomprehensible One, the AIN SUPh, the Greek apeiros, (Zohar iii. 283) was not the direct Creator of the World; but that all things have proceeded from the Primordial Source in successive Emanations, each one less excellent than the preceding, so that the universe is 'God Manifested,' and the last and remotest production is matter, a privation of perfection.

(2) That all we perceive or know of, is formed on the Sephirotic type.

(3) That human souls were pre-existent in an upper world before the origin of this present world.

(4) That human souls before incarnation dwell now in an Upper Hall, or Treasury where the decision is made as to what earth body each soul or ego shall enter.

(5)   That every soul after earth life or lives must at length be so purified as to be reabsorbed into the Infinite God.

(6)   That one human life is seldom sufficient; that two earth lives are necessary for almost all to pass; and that if failure result in the second life, a third life is passed linked with a stronger soul who draws the sinner upward into purity: this is a form of the scheme of Re-incarnation, Transmigration of souls, or Metempsychosis.

(7)   That when all the pre-existent Souls who have been incarnated here have arrived at perfection, the Evil Angels are also to be raised, and all lives will be merged into The Deity by the Kiss of Love from the Mouth of the Holy One, and the Manifested Universe shall be no more, until again vivified by the Divine FIAT.

It has been suggested by some learned authors that these Kabalistic ideas resemble those of the Alexandrian philosophy and of the Gnostics, embodying notions derived from the Pythagoreans, the Platonists and from Indian Brahmanism and Buddhism.

Let us more fully consider the conceptions of the Divinity. Isaac Myer writes :—God may be regarded from four points of view; as the Eternal One, or AIN SUP, Ain Suph; as AHIH, Aheie, I am; as IHVH, Who was, is and will be; and as ALHIM, Elohim, God in Nature, called Adonai or Lord.

In the English Old Testament the word IHVH is translated Lord, and Elohim by God: Boutell calls Jah a contraction of Jehovah.

The Jehovah of the Old Testament,--as a tribal Deity of personal characteristics, demonstrating His power and glory to a chosen people; oppressing other nations to do them service, and choosing as His special envoys and representatives men whom our civilisation would have condemned as not high enough for Spiritual power, is not represented in the Hebrew Secret Doctrine.

The Kabalah, indeed, is full of Jehovah, IHVH, the Divine Four-Lettered Name, the Tetragrammaton, but it is as the Name of a group of Divine Conceptions, of Emanations from a central Spiritual Light whose presence alone is postulated; from Absolute God there is a series of Emanations extending downward to reach Jehovah, Who is the Divine One of Binah, the Supernal Mother; other stages of Emanation lead to The Elohim, the group of Holy Spiritual attributes, associated with the Sixth Sephira, the Sun of Tiphareth.

After another manner, Jehovah is the group of the Emanations from the Deific source, called the Ten Sephiroth, "The Voices from Heaven." These Ten Sephiroth, of which the First is a condensation of the Supernal Glory from the Ain Suph Aour, the Boundless Light, appear as a Rainbow of the Divinity in a First World, or highest plane above human conception, that of Atziluth; by successive reflections, diminishing in brightness, a plane is reached which is conceivable by man, as of the purity of his highest spiritual vision. The grouping of the Ten Divine Qualities, upon this plane, into a Divine Tetrad, is symbolised by Yod Heh Vau Heh, the Tetragrammaton, the Kabalistic Jehovah, not the Yahveh of the exoteric books, but the original of that God, whose reflections of a nation's patron is formulated in the Old Testament: it is "The Ineffable Name," never pronounced, its true sound is lost, and the Jew replaces it by Adonai, ADNI; it is unpronounceable because its real vowels are unknown; it ceased to be spoken before the vowel points were introduced. (Note;--there are no extant Hebrew works with vowel points earlier than the tenth century.--A. E. WAITE.)

We find that the Kabalah contemplates a period when Chaos existed, a period of repose and absence of manifestation, when the Negative reigned supreme: this is the Pralaya of the Hindoos. From passivity there proceeded action by Emanations, and Manifested Deity arose. From Ain, repose, the Negative, proceeded Ain Suph, the No-Bound, the Limitless, the Omnipresence of the Unknowable; still condensing into manifestation through Emanation, there appears the Ain Suph Aur, "The Boundless Light," which coalescing on a point appears as

Kether, the Crown of Manifestation. Thence follow the Sephiroth, the Holy Voices, upon the Highest World; they concentrate into a divine conception, a stage of Spiritual existence which man attempts to grasp, and by defining, to limit, bound and describe, and so creates for his worship a Divine personality, his God; and the Jew named Him, --Jehovah.

By gradual stages of development, each farther from the source, there arise the powers and forces which have received the names of Archangels, Angels, Planetary Spirits, and the guardians of man; still farther from God, we obtain the human Souls, which are as Sparks of Light, struck off from the insupportable Light of Divinity, which have been formulated into Egoity to pass through a long series of changes and experiences by which they make the circuit of a Universe; they endure every stage of existence, of separation from the Divine fountain, to be at last once more indrawn to the Godhead, The Father, whence they emerged upon a pilgrimage; they follow a regular succession of evolution and involution, even as the Divine passes ever along in successive periods of outbreathing and inbreathing, of Manifestation and of Repose.

Of Divine Repose, or Chaos, the human intellect can form no conception, and only the highly spiritual man can conceive any of the sublime and exalted stages of Manifestation. To the worldly man such notions are but dreams, and any attempt to formulate them leads only to suspicions of one's sanity. To the metaphysician these ideals supply a theme of intense interest; to the theosophist they supply an illustration drawn from a foreign source of the Spiritual traditions of a long-past age, which lead one to accept the suggestion that these Spiritual conceptions are supplied from time to time by a Great Mind of another stage of existence from our own. Perhaps they are remnants of the faiths and wisdom of a long-vanished era, which had seen the life-history of races more spiritual than our own and more open to converse with the Holy Ones of higher Spiritual planes. Spiritual wisdom can only be attained by the man, or earthly being who becomes able to reach up to the sphere above; a Spiritual Being above us cannot reach down and help those who do not so purify themselves that they may be fit to rise up to the higher planes of existence.

The chief difficulty of the beginner as a student of the Kabalah, is to conquer the impressions of the reality and materiality of so-called matter. The Kabalah teaches that one must entirely relinquish the apparent knowledge of matter as an entity apart from Spirit. The assertion that matter exists, and is an entity entirely different from Spirit, and that Spirit--the God of Spirits--created it, must be denied, and the notion must be torn out by the roots before progress can be made. If matter exists, it is something, and must have come from something; but Spirit is not a thing, and creative Spirit, the highest Spiritual conception, could not make matter, the lowest thing, out of nothing: hence it is not made, and hence there is no matter. All is Spirit and conception. Ex nihilo nihil fit. All that does exist can only have come from Spirit, from Divine Essence. That Being should arise from non-being is impossible. That matter should create itself is absurd; matter cannot proceed from Spirit; the two words mean that the two ideas are entirely apart; then matter cannot exist. Hence it follows that what we call matter is but an aspect, a conception, an illusion, a mode of motion, a delusion of our physical senses.

Apart from the Kabalah, the same truth has been recognised by a few exceptional Christians and Philosophers. What is commonly known as the "Ideal Theory" was promulgated 140 years ago by Berkeley, Bishop of Cloyne in Ireland; it is nearly identical with the Kabalistic doctrine of all things being but Emanations from a Divine source, and matter but an aspect. Other philosophers have discussed the same theory in the controversy of Nominalism versus Realism: does anything exist except in name? Is there any substratum below the name of anything? Need we postulate any such basis? All is Spirit,--says the Kabalah,--and this is eternal, uncreated; intellectual and sentient on our plane; inhering are life and motion; It is self-existing, with succesive waves of action and passivity. This Spirit is the true Deity, or Infinite Being, the "Ain Suph," the Cause of all causes, and of all effects. All emanates from "That," and is in "That." The Universe is an immanent offspring of the Divine, which is manifested in a million forms of differentiation. The Universe is yet distinct from God, even as an effect is distinct from a cause; yet it is not apart from Deity, it is not a transient effect, it is immanent in the Cause. It is God made manifest to Man. Matter is our conception alone; it represents the aspect of the lowest manifestation of Spirit, or Spirit is the highest manifestation of matter. Spirit is the only substance. "Matter," says a Kabalist, "is the mere residuum of emanation, but little above non-entity." The Hindoo philosopher called matter a Maya, a delusion.

As already remarked the Supreme Being of the Kabalah is found to be demonstrated in more than one aspect. At one time the Inconceivable Eternal Power proceeding by successive Emanations into a more and more humanly conceivable existence, formulating His attributes into conceptions of Wisdom, Beauty, Power, Mercy and Governance; exhibiting these attributes first in a supernal universality beyond the ken of all spirits, angels and men, the First Word of Atziluth; then formulating a reflection of the same exalted essences on the plane of the Pure Spirits also inconceivable to man, the Second Word of Briah. Again is the reflection repeated, and the Divine Essence in its group of exalted attributes is cognisable to the Angelic Powers, the Third or Yetziratic World; and then finally the Divine abstractions of the Sacred Ten Sephiroth are by a last Emanation still more restricted and condensed than the latter, and are rendered conceivable by the Human intellect; for man exists in the Fourth World of Assiah in the shadow of the Tenth Sephira--the Malkuth, or Kingdom of the World of Shells or material objects. Small wonder then at the slightness of the ideal man can form of the Divine.

At other times we find the metaphysical abstract laid aside, and all the wealth of Oriental imagery lavished on the description of God; imagery although grouped and clustered around the emblem of an exalted humanity, yet so inflated, so extravagantly magnified, that the Heavenly man is lost sight of in the grandeur and tenuity of the word painting of the Divine portrait. Divine anthropomorphism it may be, but an anthropomorphism so tenuous by means of its grandeur, that the human elements affording the bases of the analogy quite disappear in the Heavenly Man of their divine reveries.

Permit me to afford to you an example of one sublime, deific dream:--

"In this conformation He is known; He is the Eternal of the Eternal ones; the Ancient of the Ancient ones; the Concealed of the Concealed ones; in His symbols He is knowable although He is unknowable. White are His garments, and His appearance is as a Face, vast and terrible in its vastness. Upon a throne of flaming brilliance is He seated, so that he may direct its flashing Rays. Into many thousand worlds the brightness of His face is extended, and from the Light of this brightness the just shall receive worlds of joy and reward in the existence to come. Within His skull exist daily a thousand myriads of worlds; all draw their existence from Him, and by Him are upheld. From that Head distilleth a Dew, and from that Dew which floweth down upon the worlds, are the dead raised up in the lives and on the worlds to come."

The God of the Kabalah is "Infinite Existence": He cannot be defined as the "Assemblage of Lives," nor is he truly the "totality of his attributes." Yet without deeming all lives to be of Him, and His attributes to be universal, He cannot be known by man. He existed before He caused the Emanations of H is essence to be demonstrated, He was before all that exists is, before all lives on our plane, or the plane above, or the World of pure Spirits, or the Inconceivable existence; but then He resembled nothing we can conceive, and was Ain Suph, and in the highest abstraction Ain, alone, Negative Existence.

Yet before the manifest became demonstrated, all existence was in him; the Known preexisted in the Unknown, Who is the "Ancient of Days."

But it is not this dream-like aspect of poetic phantasy exhibited in the Kabalah that I can further bring to your notice. Let us return to the Philosophic view of the attributes of Deity, which is the keynote of the whole of the doctrine.

The primary human conception of God is then the Passive state of Negative Existence AIN--not active; from this the mind of man passes to conceive of AIN SUPh, of God as the Boundless, the Unlimited, Undifferentiated, Illimitable One; and the third stage is AIN SUPh AUR--Boundless Light, Universal Light--"Let there be Light" was formulated, and "There was Light." The Passive has put on Activity; the Conscious God has awaked. Let us now endeavour to conceive of the concentration of this effulgence, let us formulate a gathering together of the rays of this illumination into a Crown of glorified radiance, and we recognise KTR, Kether, the Crown, the First Sephira, First Emanation of Incomprehensible Deity, the first conceivable attribute of immanent manifested Godhead: also named ADM OILAH, Adam Oilah, The Heavenly Man, and Autik Yomin, The Ancient of days. The devout Rabbi bows his head and adores the sublime conception. He is represented in the Hebrew Old Testament by the Divine Name AHIH, Aheieh, "I am " (Exodus iii. v. 4).

The conscious God having arisen in His energy, there follow immediately two further Emanations, the Trio shining in the symbol of a radiant triangle. ChKMH, Chokmah, Wisdom, The King, with the Divine Name IH, Jah is the Second Sephira; BINH, Binah, Understanding, The Queen, and the Divine Name IHVH Jehovah is the Third Sephira,--the Supernal Triad" is demonstrated.

Then follow GDULH, Gedulah, also called CHSD, Chesed, Mercy, with the Divine Name AL, El; and its contrast GBURH, Geburah, Severity, also called Pachad, Fear, with the Divine Name ALH, Eloah; and the reflected triangle is completed by the Sixth Sephira, the Sun, named TPART, Tiphareth, or Beauty, with the name ALHIM Elohim; considered as a triangle of reflection with the apex below. The third triangle may be considered as a second reflection with the apex below; it is formed of the seventh, eighth, and ninth Sephiroth; NTzCh, Netzach, Firmness or Victory, with the name Jehovah Sabaoth; HUD, Hod or Hud, Splendour, with the name Elohim Sabaoth; and ISUD, Yesod, Foundation, with the name AL ChAI, El Chai.

Finally, all these ideals are resumed in a single form, the Tenth Sephira, MLKUT, Malkuth, the Shekinah, the Kingdom, also sometimes called Tzedek, Righteousness. The whole Decad form "Adam Kadmon," "The Archetypal Man," and the wondrous OTz ChIIM, "Tree of Life." In the ancient figures of Adam Kadmon we see Kether, the Crown, over the forehead; Chokmah and Binah are the two halves of the thinking brain; Gedulah and Geburah are the organs of action, the right and left upper limbs; Tiphareth

is the heart and the vital organs of the chest; Netzach and Hud are the lower limbs right and left; Jesod refers to the digestive and reproductive organs and abdomen; and lastly Malkuth is compared to the feet as a basis or foundation of man upon this earth or lowest plane: see the plate of The Adam Kadmon, Archetypal Man, or The First Adam.

These Triads were looked upon as formed of a Principle of Union and a male and female potency, and thus a Balance, MTQLA, Methequela, exists.

Almost as old as the Kabalistic doctrine of the Sephiroth, the Intelligences, or Emanations, are the peculiar forms in which they were represented in diagrams which resume all Kabalistic ideas, and are emblems of these views on every subject. Every Deific conception can be thus demonstrated, and also the constitution of the Angelic Hosts, the principles of Man's Nature, the group of Planetary Bodies, the Metallic elements, the Zigzag flash of the Lightning and the composition of the sacred Tetragrammaton, the Mystical Jehovah, IHVH, Yod, Heh, Vau, Heh, numbering 26. See Plates I., II., III., IV., V., and VI. This Decad of Deific Emanations is to be conceived as first formulated on the Divine First plane of Atziluth, which is entirely beyond our ken; to be reproduced on the Second plane of pure Spirit, Briah; to exist in the same Decad form in the world of Yetzirah, the Third or Formative plane; and finally to be sufficiently condensed as to be cognizable by the human intellect on the Fourth plane of Assiah, on which we seem to exist. From our point of view we may regard the "Tree of Life" as a type of many divine processes and forms of manifestation, but these are symbols we use to classify our ideals, and we must not debase the divine Emanations by asserting these views of the Sephiroth are real, but only as conceivable by humanity.

For example, the Kabalah demonstrates the grouping of the Ten Sephiroth into Three Pillars; the Pillar of Mercy, the Pillar of Severity, and the Pillar of Mildness between them: these may also be associated with the Three Mother Letters, A, M, Sh; Aleph, Mem and Shin. Then again by two horizontal lines we may form three groups and consider these Sephiroth to become types of the Three divisions of Man's Nature, the Intellectual, Moral, and Sensuous (neglecting Malkuth, the material body), thus connecting the Kabalah with Mental and

Moral Philosophy and Ethics. By three lines again we consider the Sephiroth to be divisible into Four Planes., upon each of which I have already said you must conceive the whole Ten Sephiroth to be immanent. By a series of Six lines we group them into Seven planes referable to the worlds of the Seven Planetary powers, thus connecting the Kabalah with Astrology. (W. Gorn Old has recently published a volume called "Kabalistic Astrology.")

To each Sephira were allotted in Briah an especial Archangel, and in Yetzirah an army of Angels; these connect the Kabalah with Talismanic Magic. There is also a close relation between the old Kabalistic theology and Alchymy; each Sephira of Assiah becomes the allegoric emblem of one of the metals: and there is a special Rabbinic volume named "Asch Metzareph" entirely concerned with Alchymy; its name in English meaning is "Cleansing Fires." (My English translation can be obtained.) A. E. Waite in his work on the Kabalah states that Rabbi Azariel ben Menachem in his "Commentary on the Sephiroth" allots a particular colour to each one, but these do not agree with the colours given in the Zohar, where we find Kether called colourless, Tiphareth purple, and Malkuth sapphire-blue.

These Ten Sephiroth are thought of as being connected together by "Paths," Twenty-two in number, shown on the Diagram; they are numbered by means of the letters of the Hebrew Alphabet, each of which being equally a letter and a number. The 22 Trumps of the pack of Tarot cards (Tarocchi) are also related to these Paths. The 22 Paths, added to the 10 Sephiroth form the famous "Thirty-two Ways" by which Wisdom descends by successive stages upon Man, and may enable him to mount to the Source of Wisdom by passing successively upward through these 32 Paths. This process of mental Abstraction was the Rabbinic form of what the Hindoo knows as Yoga, or the Union of the human with the Divine, by contemplation and absorption of the mind in a mystical reverie.

Frequently quoted Kabalistic words are: Arikh Anpin, Makroprosopos, the Vast Countenance which is a title of Kether the Crown, Deity Supreme; Zauir Anpin, Mikroprosopos, the Lesser Countenance is the Central Sun, Tiphereth, a conception that has something in common with that of the Christian Christ, the Son of God. (The former was represented by a face in profile, the latter by the full face. M. Mathers). Binah is the Supernal Mother, Aima. Malkuth is the Inferior Mother, the Bride of the Mikroprosopos. Daath or Knowledge is the union of Chokmah and Binah, of wisdom and understanding. Merkabah was the Chariot Throne of God of the vision of Ezekiel mentioned in his chapters i. and x.; it rested on wheels and was carried by Four Cherubim, the Sacred Animal Forms, which resembled the Man, Lion, Bull and Eagle, which were related to the Four quarters of the World, and to Four types of humanity.

The Four Letters Yod, He, Vau, He, or as we say IHVH, of the name we call Jehovah, are allotted and distributed by the Kabalistic doctrine among the Sephiroth in a peculiar manner, forming the mysterious conception of the Tetragrammaton, that awful name of Divine Majesty which might never be uttered by the common people, and whose true pronunciation has been for many centuries confessedly lost to the Jews and has never been known to the Christians.

The views of the Kabalists on Cosmogony are not easy to explain, but as before said the Supreme Boundless God, the "Ain Suph" was not the direct Creator of the World, nor was the world made out of nothing.

The highest Trinity of "The Crown, King and Queen" having arisen by Divine Emanation, its powers descended and expanded into the Seven Lower Sephiroth, and produced the Universe in their own image, a decad of forces, as a whole constituting the ADM QDMUN Adam Quadmun, or Adam Kadmon, the Primordial or Archetypal Man; the world produced is the existing Universe of which we have cognizance. The universe is called the "Garment of God": this lower world is a copy of the Divine World, everything here has its prototype above. (Zohar ii. 20.)

Some Kabalistic treatises speak of earlier worlds created before the conjunction of the Divine King and Queen; these perished in the void; these lost worlds are referred to in Genesis 36, v. 31-40, as "The Kings of Edom who reigned before Israel," they are said to have perished one after the other; these worlds were convulsed and were no more known.

Having considered the Divine Emanations, and the origin of the Universe, I must refer to the spiritual beings of the Four Worlds. In the First purest and highest World of Atziluth there dwell only the Primary Ten Sephiroth of the Adam Oilah or Archetype, perfect and immutable.

In the Second World of Briah reside the Archangels headed by "Metatron" related to Kether, in solemn grandeur; He is the garment of Al Shaddai, the visible manifestation of God; the Number of both is 314 (Zohar iii. 231a). The word Metatron meant "The Great Teacher." It has a curious resemblance to the Greek words met thronon, beside or beneath the throne of God; but this derivation is fanciful. He rules the other Archangels of the Universe, who govern in their courses all the heavenly bodies, and the evolutions of the dwellers on them: He is, according to the Kabalists, the efficient God of our

Earth,--the Greek Demiourgos. The other Arch-Angels are according to Macgregor Mathers, Ratziel, Tzaphkiel, Tzadquiel, Kamael, Michael, Haniel, Raphael, Gabriel, and Sandalphon.

In the Third World of Yetzirah are the Ten hosts of Angelic beings, a separate class for each Sephira; they are intelligent incorporeal beings, clothed in a garment of light, and are set over the several heavenly bodies, the planets, over the elemental forces, and over seasons, times, etc.; they are the officers of the great Arch-Angels. The Hosts of Angels of the Sephiroth are Chaioth ha kodesh, Auphanim, Arelim, Chashmalim, Seraphim, Melakim, Elohim, Beni Elohim, Cherubim, and tenthly the Ishim who are the Beatified Souls of men and women.

The Fourth World of Assiah is filled with the lowest beings, the Evil Demons, Kliphoth or Qliphoth, the cortices or shells, and with all so-called material objects, and to this world belong men, the Egos or Souls imprisoned in earthly human bodies. This world also has its ten grades, each one more far from the higher forces and forms, each one more dark and impure. First come THU, Tohu, the Formless; and BHU, Bohu, the Void, thirdly ChShK, the Darkness, of the early universe, and from these our world was developed and now exists; then come seven hells, whose dwellers are evil beings representing all human sins; their rulers are Samael or Satan the angel of death, and Lilith, the Asheth Zenunim, the Woman of whoredom, and this pair of demons are also called "The Beast," see Zohar ii. 255; Samael had also an incommunicable name, which was IHVH reversed; for Demon est Deus inversus.

The whole universe only became complete with the creation of Man, called the Microcosm, the Earthly Adam; a copy of "The Archetypal Man" after another manner; he has principles and faculties and forms comparable to all the Sephiroth and Worlds, although his material body dwells on the Assiatic plane.

From God, the Angels and the World, let us pass to consider more fully what the Kabalah teaches about Man, the human Soul or Ego.

It has already been explained that the Doctrine of Emanation postulates successive stages of the manifestation of the Supreme Spirit, which may be regarded as existing on separate planes. Now the Ten Sephiroth condense their energy into a formulated Four-parted group of Three Spiritual planes, and a plane of so-called Objectivity, or of Matter. These Ten Sephiroth, and the planes, each contribute an essence which in their totality, in ever-varying proportion, constitutes Man. At his origin there was formulated what the scientists might call "Archetypal Man," and what the Kabalists named Adam Kadmon, ADM QDMUN. Primeval Man, the Greek protogonos. Successive stages of beings of this type pass along the ages through a descending scale, offering the individual every variety of experience, and then along an ascending scale of redevelopment until human perfection is attained, and ultimate reunion with the Divine is the result of the purified Soul having completed its pilgrimage.

Before we consider Man in his present state we must note the views of the Kabalah upon Man in his primal state.

Man was the final Word of Creation, he was a resume of all forms, and so transcended the angels in his faculties. The first man had no fleshy body, no material envelope: Adam and Eve were clothed only in ethereal forms, and were not subject to appetites or passions, they dwelled in Light in the GN OiDN, Garden of Aidin, of Eden, of pleasant peace (Zohar ii. 229b). The man and the woman before their descent to this world were as one,--androgynous; at incarnation they were separated into sexes. The first human pair broke the first commandment, they sinned and were doomed to a complete descent into matter; the Lord God made them "coats of skin," He gave them material bodies, and with these came the need of food, and the passions required to bring forth a succession of earthly bodies.

Yet man is still the copy of God on earth; his form is related to the Tetragrammaton of Jehovah IHVH, for in a diagram, Yod is as the head, Heh the arms, Vau the body, and the final Heh the lower limbs: (see Zohar ii. 42a). The first pair were tempted by Samael, the allegorical Personality of the lower tendencies, which give the craving to experience earth life and take a part in its continuous changes of force and form. They did what they knew would imperil their purely psychic existence, they sank fully into material forms, they took on the grossness of Malkuth, and so were separated from the Sephirotic Tree, from the Higher Potencies, which have no taint of matter. All matter is ever changing its form, and so their bodies must be changed; their bodies died, and so must the bodies of all incarnated Egos; at death the personality passes away to a rest, and then to a further experience of life, or to a sphere of punishment, or to a realm of bliss.

In their earthly forms they brought forth bodies like their own, and God sent down other souls to dwell in them, to experience earth life, its sins and sufferings; and to pass a probation by which they also might fall, but yet may rise to regain a share of man's lost estate and finally to rise up through the Sephiroth to a reunion with the Divine Essence.

Remember that the Sephirotic Crown was First, then came Chokmah, a masculine Potency, and then Binah, a feminine one; from their union arose the created universe of angels, men and earth: but 'as above so below,' so we have in Genesis a Man formed, then succeeds a Woman, and from them all others.

In the " Commentary on the Creation of Genesis," still allegorical like Genesis itself, it is stated :-- "There is in Heaven a treasury called GUP, Guph, and all the Souls which were created in the beginning, and hereafter to come into this world, The Holy One placed therein: out of this treasury The Holy One furnishes children in the womb with Souls."

A further commentary in symbolic language narrates how The Holy One perceiving a child's body to be in formation, sends for a suitable Ego to inhabit it.

"The Holy One, blessed be He, beckons to an Angel who is set over the disembodied souls, and says to him, 'Bring me such a soul': and this is being always done since the world began; the soul appears before the Holy One and worships in His presence, to whom the Eternal One says :--'Betake thyself to this form.' Instantly the soul excuses himself, saying, 'Oh Governor of the World, I am satisfied with the world in which I have been so long: if it please Thee, do not force me into this foul body, for I am a Spirit.' The Holy One, blessed be He, answers: 'The world I am about to send thee into is needed for thee, it is to pass down through it that I formed thee from myself.' And so the soul is forced to incarnate and sink into the world where matter will imprison him, where he must suffer, but where he may overcome and from whence he must rise again. The Zohar adds the statement: "and whatever the man learns and displays on earth life, he knew before his incarnation."

This is a parallel doctrine to the Buddhist scheme of Re-incarnation with Karma as God-eternal law, relentlessly compelling the individual Ego to a new earth life.

Christian Ginsburg states that a "Transmigration of Souls" was the belief of the Pharisees in the time of Josephus; and this dogma was held by many Jews up to the ninth century of our era. The Caraite Jews have accepted it ever since the seventh century. St. Jerome says it was a doctrine of the early Christian Church taught only to a select few believers, and Origen was of opinion that without transmigration, the incidents of the struggle between Esau and Jacob before birth, Genesis 25, v. 22, and the reference to Jeremiah in the mother's womb could not be explained, Jer. i. 5.

The Kabalah then teaches that the Egos have come out from the Spirit Fountain, suffer incarnation again and again until experience and perfection have been attained, and ultimately rejoin the Divine Source: Zohar i. 145, 168; ii. 97.

Now what is it that dwells for a time in this 'Coat of Skin," as Genesis in chapter 3, v. 21, calls it, this so-called material body? It is a Divine Spark, composed of several elements derived from the symbolic Four Parts of Jehovah, and from Three Worlds, and these are seated in the Fourth World of Effects, the Material Universe. Now it is no doubt true that in the several Kabalistic schools, the numbers and names of these Essences vary, but the basal idea remains the same: just in a similar way the principles of Man's constitution, as stated in different Hindoo books, also vary, but the root idea is the same in them all.

The Human Principles may be stated as Three in a fourth--the body; or as Five, recognising Astral form and material body; or as Seven, subdividing the divine principle; or as Ten, comparable to the Sephiroth. To explain these fully would take a long essay and would require many Hebrew abstruse words, a difficulty to those who are unused to them: two systems will suffice as an illustration.

From Yod, the Je of Jehovah, comes the highest over-shadowing of the Divine, comparable to the Atma of the Indian philosophies. From He, the ho of Jehovah, comes Neshamah, the Buddhi of the Hindoos, the spiritual soul. From Vau, the v of Jehovah, comes Ruach, the Manas of the Hindoos, Intellect and Mind. From the final He, the ah of Jehovah, is derived Nephesh, the Kama of the Hindoos, the appetites and passions.

These are all implanted in the Astral shell, which moulds the physical body, the instrument which acts upon material objects.

The Human Soul is again conceived of as distributed through several distinct forms of conscious manifestation related to the "Ten Sephiroth": the several Kabalistic treatises give several groupings, which are all relevant one to the other, the most usual one being a triple division, into Nephesh, the passions referred to Malkuth; Ruach, the Mind, Reason, and Intellect referred to the group of Six Sephiroth lying around the Sun of Tiphereth; and Neshamah, the spiritual aspirations associated with the Supernal Triangle of the Queen, King and Crown.

These Human principles function upon Four Worlds,--Divine, Moral, Intellectual and Emotional respectively: and either of these essences may dominate a man, and they do, in fact, exist in constantly varying proportions. The highest principle overshadows the others, and the central ones may reach up to the higher; or by neglect of opportunities, or by vicious actions, may fall lower and lower, so as to approximate to the seeming matter of the body. As the Neshamah draws one to Spiritual excellence, so the Nephesh leads down to physical enjoyment.

In another form of symbolism the Kabalist tells us a man has two companions, or guides; one on the right, Yetzer ha Tob, to good acts, he is from the higher Sephiroth; and one on the left, Yetzer ha Ra, encouraging the appetites and passions, temptations to evil, is an agent of Samael and of The Beast. Man is in a very unfortunate position according to the Zohar 95 b, for it is there said that the Evil Angel joins him at birth, but the Good Angel only at the age of 13 years.

As to Death, as we have already learned, the man's Ego or Soul, unless the life has been superexcellent, has to be re-born in another form, but at death, as all religions agree, great changes occur. According to the Kabalah, the visible material body, the Guph, decays, and the Animal aspect of the soul, the Nephesh, only gradually fades away from it: the Ruach, the Human aspect, passes away from the Assiatic plane, and the Neshamah, the spiritual soul, returns to the Treasury of Heaven, to the Gan Oidin, or of Paradise, perfected to a Spiritual world beyond the plain of rebirths. The "Sepher jareh chattaim" says that a man is judged in the same hour in which he dies; for the Shekinah, a Presence of the Divine One, comes near him, with three Angels, of whom the chief is Dumah, the Angel of Silence: if the soul is condemned, Dumah takes it to

Gai-Hinnom, or hell, for a period of punishment before the next incarnation; if approved, the Soul passes to an Oidin or Heaven. In the end of the present manifestation of the Universe, all souls will have become perfected by suffering, have been blessed in Paradise, and will be in reunion with the God from Whom they came forth.

The Kabalistic theory of man's constitution, origin and destiny is very different from the modern Christian view, but differs from the Indian schemes more in manner of presentation than in principle, and these two may be fitly studied side by side and each will illuminate the other. There is, indeed, no sharp line of cleavage between the Western mystic doctrines, the Kabalism of the Middle Ages related to the Egyptian Hermeticism, and the Indian Esoteric Theosophy. They differ in language nomenclature, and in the imagery employed in the effort to represent spiritual ideas to mankind; but there is no sufficient reason for any condemnation of either school by any other. The world of intellectual culture is wide enough for both to exist side by side, and the mere fact that they are philosophic Systems in any way comprehensible to men is evidence that either can be composed of pure and unveiled truth, for we are still only able to see as in a glass darkly, and must make much further progress before we can hope to see God face to face and know Him as He is.

We must be content to progress, as students have ever done, by stages of development; in each grade the primal truths are re-stated in a different form; they are revealed or reveiled in language and symbolism suitable to the learner's own mental condition; hence the need of a teacher, of a guide who has traversed the path, and who can recognise by personal communion the stage which each pupil has attained. There is no royal or easy path to high attainment in Mysticism. Unwearied effort, combined with purity of life, is of vital importance. The human intellect can only appreciate and assimilate that which the mind's eye can at any time perceive. The process cannot be forced. Mystic lore cannot be stolen. If any learner did appropriate the knowledge of a Grade beyond him it would be to him but folly, disappointment and darkness.

Students have often been offered a doctrine, or assertion, or explanation, which their intellect has rejected as absurd, or as sheer superstition; which same dogma they have later in life assimilated with every feeling of esteem. Occultism in this resembles Freemasonry; we are either admitted to the hidden knowledge, or we are not; and if we are not admitted, we never believe any secret of its ritual even if it be offered to us. The secrets of Occultism are like Freemasonry; in truth they are to some extent the secrets that Freemasonry has lost. They are of their very nature inviolable; for they can only be attained by personal progress; they might be plainly told to the outsider, and not be understood by him. For if anyone has been able to divine and to grasp such a secret, he will not tell it even to his dearest friend; for the simple reason that if his friend is unable to divine it for himself, its communication in mere words would not confer the hidden knowledge upon him.

The whole Kabalistic theories are of a nature similar to the secrets of Freemasonry; there was much doctrine that was never written nor printed: these works often describe imagery which seems folly, and contain doctrines that at first seem absurd; yet they enshrine the highly spiritual teachings which I have shortly outlined. The mere reading of these volumes is of little avail; the spiritual eye needs to be opened to see spiritual things; and the great Kabalists of old did not cast pearls of wisdom before the ignorant or the vicious, nor suffer the unclean to enter the Temple of Wisdom. The serious student must make strenuous efforts to attain to the higher life of the True Occultism, then perchance in a distant future, a record of temptations avoided, and of a life of self-sacrifice may serve as Signs and Pass Words to secure admission to the Palace of the Great King.

Copyright © 2023 by SSEL
Scribere Semper Et Legere
Ebook ISBN 979-10-299-1545-1
Paperback ISBN 979-10-299-1546-8
Cover Design : Canva.com
All rights reserved.

www.ingramcontent.com/pod-product-compliance
Lightning Source LLC
LaVergne TN
LVHW030344070526
838199LV00067B/6434